BOROUGH of POOLE

POOLE
A Pictorial History

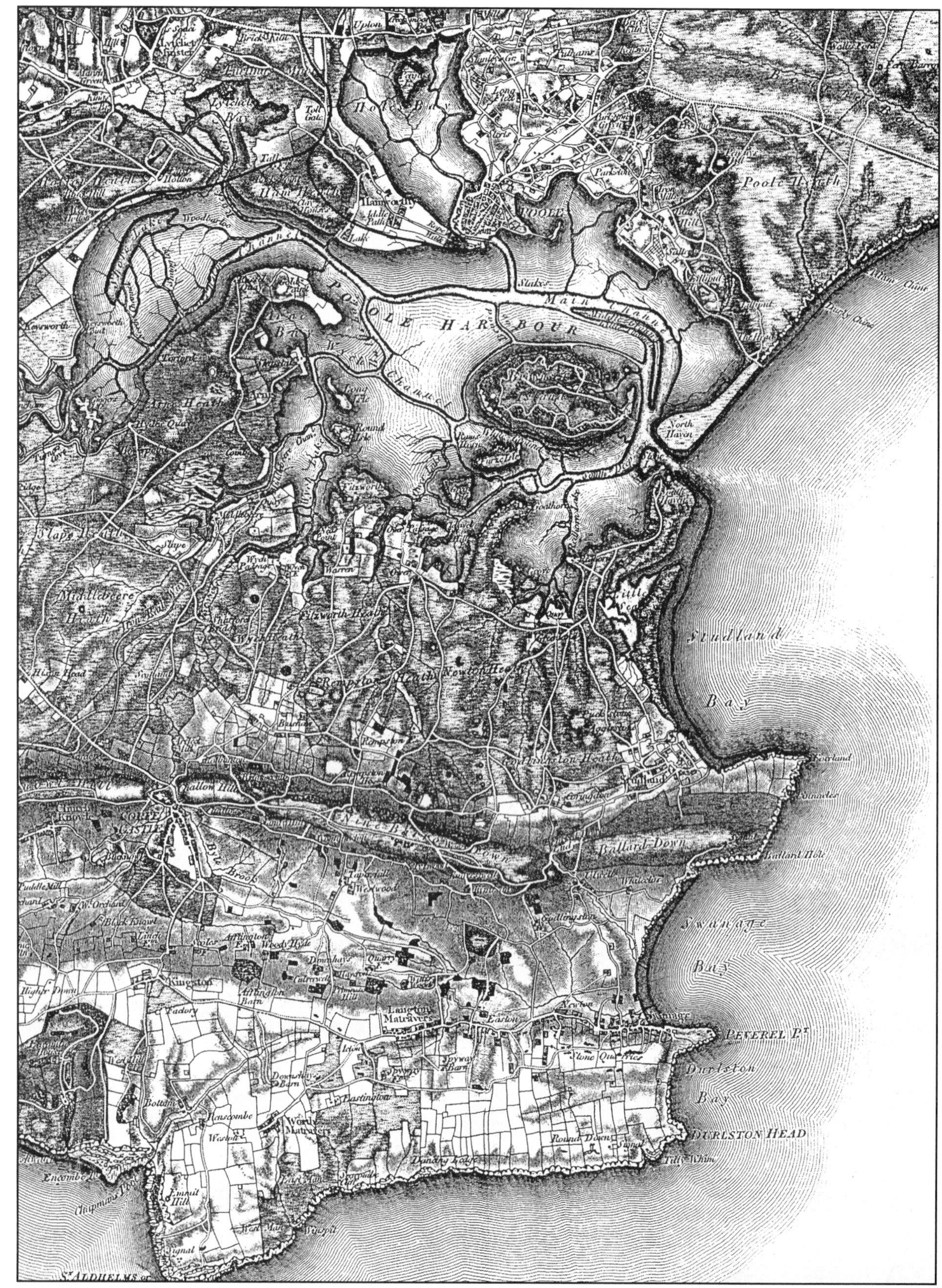

1811 Ordnance Survey Map with 1847 additions

POOLE
A Pictorial History

Ian Andrews

Phillimore

1994

Published by
PHILLIMORE & CO. LTD.,
Shopwyke Manor Barn, Chichester, West Sussex

ISBN 0 85033 948 0

Printed and bound in Great Britain by
BIDDLES LTD.
Guildford, Surrey

To the memory of Poole's recent past

Poole Generating Station is now a cleared site awaiting 'regeneration'. It took from 1948 to 1953 to build and produced enough power for 400,000 homes. The design was approved by the Royal Fine Art Commission. Fly ash from the original coal burning station was dumped at Turlin Moor to create playing fields, but before complete reclamation the station converted to oil and the fly ash had to be reduced in depth to complete the whole area. The chimneys, 325 ft in height, were landmarks visible for miles around to mariners and others as a sign one was approaching Poole. They were demolished in February 1993 on the author's last day of work as the last bewigged and gowned Town Clerk of Poole; an office that had been in existence since 1558 with its own oath of office requiring the holder to 'keep the secrets of the Town and not to extend the same other than to such as are sworn to the Town'.

List of Illustrations

Frontispiece: 1811 Ordnance Survey Map

Acknowledgements

Compiling this collection was fun, but it was only possible with the help of others. I wish to thank all those who have generously helped me by lending material, readily giving permission for it to be reproduced or sharing their knowledge or facilities. I apologise to those whose material was not used on this occasion, but I had to make a selection trying, where possible, to avoid postcards or material more suitable for other publications in favour of the 'one off' picture, even if the photographic standard is less than perfect.

In particular I would mention Mrs M. Beamish, 'Rocky' Bendall, Dorset County Library Service (Poole Local History Collection), Dorset County Record Office, Miss Y. Glover, Gordon Handcock, Cyril Hart, Frank Henson, John Hillier, Mrs. I. M. Hoare, Mrs. C. Hopkinson, Bob Hucklesby, Messrs Laceys, Leading Seaman Lucas, Poole Arts Trust Ltd., Poole Borough Museum Service (including Poole Borough Archives), fellow Trustees of Poole Historical Trust, Poole Maritime Trust, Poole Tourism Service, Provincial Museum of Newfoundland and Labrador, Graham Smith, Mrs. A. Swain, Trinity Museum (Nfld.), fellow Trustees of Trinity Trust, US Navy Historical Centre, Mrs. S. Viney, Miss P. Wilnecker and the late Viscount Wimborne.

I apologise if any other copyright ownership exists of which I am not aware or which I have not been able to trace.

Above all I thank my wife, Valerie, for having encouraged me to indulge in the pleasant pastime of recording the past as a healthy antidote to the pressures of the present.

IAN ANDREWS

Introduction

As you bask in the sun on Sandbanks beach the last thing you think of is history. Its eight consecutive 'blue flags' may yet earn it a place in the annals. Yet beneath your feet prehistory was laying down the future of the area. The Alps had been forced upwards in gigantic upheavals and glaciers had cut great channels. The melting of the last ice cut the south coast off from the Continent. It left the great basin with 96 miles of coast that we now know as Poole. Its proximity to the Isle of Wight made its tides different. It is the world's largest natural harbour served by double tides. Beneath it lay clay- and oil-bearing beds that were later to be exploited. Beside it scrub and trees, gorse and heather grew, the bleak Egdon of Hardy. The existence of flints indicates man's presence in the Bronze Age as a hunter, especially along the Stour Valley. Not until the Iron Age is there evidence of the first use of the water for transport. A log boat dated *c*.395 B.C., dredged from the harbour in 1964, and carved from a single oak tree is the precious reminder.

Romans occupied Hamworthy, for whom it was a supply port known as Moriconium. Roman coins, a pottery and a mill have all been discovered and it may have been the base for salt panning. The road from Hamworthy led to a junction at Badbury Rings with the route from Old Sarum to Dorchester and the route north into Cranborne Chase. Tin from Cornwall was brought to the port and exported to the Cotentin peninsula, the nearest part of the kingdom of Gaul.

The Anglo-Saxon Chronicle frequently mentions Fromemouth, which is Poole harbour, but the embanked and fortified town of Wareham, stronghold of the West Saxons, was the target of the Danes. In 789 three Danish ships burned Wareham; a fate which was repeated many times. Alfred the Great trapped the Danish fleet in the shallow waters behind Arne in 876, and drove it down past Poole and out of the harbour in a running fight. A great storm was raging at the time which caught the Danes when they reached the open sea. Of their ships 120 were wrecked on the shore near Studland. When Canute came to take the crown, he occupied Brownsea Island and made it his storage place for the loot he took from the abbey at Arne.

Wareham was proving unsafe in times of war and was a long way from the open sea. Either because of the almost complete destruction of Wareham and its fortifications during the civil war between the rival factions of Stephen and Matilda in the first part of the 12th century, or because the river approach was silting up and the size of vessels was increasing, more use came to be made of the deeper channels of Poole. There vessels could ride in safety and load or discharge cargoes. As Leland wrote in the 16th century, Poole 'no town of auncient occupying in marchantdise: but rather of old tyme a poore fisshar villagge ... little by little increased to its present bigness'.

In 1200, just after he came to the throne, John visited Canford of which Poole formed part, but it is unlikely he came again in his later years, for the lord of the manor of Canford and Poole was one of those who stood round him at Runnymede in 1215 and made him sign the Magna Carta (Great Charter) which promised liberty to the people of England. The manor was in the hands of the earls of Salisbury, descendants of the lords of Montacute to whom William the Conqueror had granted vast estates in the western counties. The family were great fighters. One, William Longespee, was tall and used a long sword; he took his name from his weapon. It was he who granted to 'Lapole' a weekly market on Tuesdays and a yearly fair on the vigil and feast of St Margaret and the two days following (19 to 22 July). This was Poole's earliest charter.

The earls of Salisbury were an unfortunate family, many of whom were killed or executed rather than dying in their beds. Their example of opposition to greedy and oppressive kings was not lost on the people of Poole, who throughout the ages have battled against oppression.

By 1248 Poole had become a busy community which felt the lordship of Canford was a hindrance to trade. They paid 70 marks (£46 13s. 4d.) to free the town from William Longespee II's rights. It was to be a shrewd investment. Henceforth the burgesses of Poole could levy their own duties on shipping, hold their own courts for the governance of the town, cut turves on the heath, and the port reeve (or mayor) could deal with foreign shipping and merchandise.

The rise in Poole's shipping in the 13th century is evidenced by the number of writs from the King to supply him with ships or to stop or resume trade with France. When war began again in 1295 the sheriffs of Dorset had orders to take to La Pole 1,000 quarters of wheat, 300 quarters of oats, 200 quarters of beans, 300 'bacons' and 10,000 or 12,000 'of the fish called hake' to be conveyed to Guernsey. About this time the Town Cellars or King's Woolhouse (now known as Scaplen's Court) was built.

Demands for shipping for the King's wars were repeated many times but the people of Poole preferred to mind their own affairs and let the clerks from London punish the port. On more than one occasion measures of enforcement were suffered, even though more money could be made in the King's service at 3d. a day than could be gained by fishing. However, in 1347 at the siege of Calais, the key to the conquest of France, the town had four ships and 94 men present. The inhabitants of Poole were also prepared for war on land as they took part in compulsory archery practice (at West Butts Street) after divine service on Sundays.

After Calais the town, in common with most of England, fell on hard times. In 1348 it rained almost every day from Midsummer to Christmas. Crops were ruined and from France, through Weymouth and sweeping Dorset, came the dreaded plague—the Black Death. Poole was almost ruined. The dead were buried in their hundreds at Baiter.

Poole sent two members to Westminster for the first time in 1341. In 1371 William of Montacute, Earl of Salisbury, who had distinguished himself in battle at Crecy and Poitiers, granted the town additional rights, in particular those of cutting turf and furze on his great heath for firing. He also confirmed the port reeve as 'Admiral of the Port of Poole', a title still enjoyed as a courtesy. The boundaries of Poole's waters were indicated in the Winchelsea Certificate dated 26 April 1364 granted by the Mayor of Winchelsea, itself one of the Cinque Ports.

Poole was a port of embarkation for pilgrims making their way to the shrine of St James at Santiago. The *James* of Poole took 80 pilgrims on each trip. By 1434 the King was granting over 2,400 licences for this pilgrimage and the numbers from Poole were so great that it adopted three scallop shells, the sign of a Compostella pilgrim, for its arms. The dolphin (the marine equivalent of the lion as king of the beasts) represented the fishing industry.

The south coast was under attack from Brittany in the early 15th century. The hour brought forward the man to lead the English in reprisals, a native of Poole known as Harry Paye. Charged with piracy at the behest of the French, the authorities winked at his misdeeds and empowered him to harass the French, who had burnt Portland. He raided 40 Normandy towns and villages, swept across the Bay of Biscay and on Finisterre carried away the crucifix as loot. In 1405 a reprisal fleet of Spanish and French ships entered Poole. It was unfortified and Paye was away. Poole men drove back the Spanish but the French then joined in. The townspeople covered their retreat using doors as shields. Arrows flew so thick and fast that those who had armour 'looked as if they had been feathered with them'. The church was burnt, but the town was too hot to hold and the invaders retreated, killing Paye's brother. Two years later, to prove he had not forgotten Poole men's valour and as compensation, Paye brought 120 French merchant prizes, laden with wine, salt and iron, into the harbour.

In 1433 Henry VI declared that Melcombe, his customs port, was not sufficiently strong to protect goods. Recognising that the town of Poole was notably populous and safe, he created it a port with the rights of Staple at a time when British wool was much in demand. He also licensed the crenellation and fortification of the town. The powerful fraternity of St George, a religious guild, was founded in Poole about 1400. It came to possess a considerable amount of property, most of which was to be purchased by the corporation after 1547, when it was confiscated by the Crown during the Reformation. The guild supported the church of St James and also built an almshouse in the town.

In 1453 the market day was changed to Thursday and two annual fairs were granted by Henry VI, but it was a later king, Richard III, who appeared to favour the town most of all by starting to build a piece of the town wall at one end of the quay. He 'promised large thingges to the toun of Pole'. In return he seemed to have wanted money for in 1454 Poole was expected to find a subsidy of £40 towards the expenses of the royal household, and in 1482 the sum of £100. In 1483 Henry of Richmond, afterwards Henry VII, came to England to try to take the crown. He appeared off South Haven, having been separated from companion ships in a storm, and would have landed at Poole but for the opposition of the townspeople, who were loyally disposed to accept whatever King Richard had promised.

The voyage of Cabot from Bristol in 1497, during which he touched shore in Newfoundland and discovered its fishing potential, was to prove of great significance to Poole. Merchants and fishermen were to follow his route and make fortunes in a trade in which Poole became pre-eminent and which supported its economy for three hundred years. The Golden Age of Poole was dawning.

The reputation of Poole shipbuilders led Henry VIII to commandeer its shipwrights in 1512 to build his vessel *Henry Grace de Dieu*. Canford manor was then in Henry's hands and he licensed the town windmill at Baiter and a reservoir at Tatnam to supply water. He also created St James' church a 'royal peculiar', separate from Canford. The town built a blockhouse on Brownsea, and he provided arms and ammunition.

Claiming prize-money for capturing foreign ships was better than steady work. The men were all at sea and Lord Russell wrote, 'never was such things seen before—all the fishing fleets were manned by women'. The wool trade had declined and the town so neglected itself that in Elizabeth's time 'the havens, ditches, walls, church, quay and other places are very chargeable to be kept in repair'. Apart from Brownsea the town's defences against the Armada threat were few. Its population was recorded in a 1574 census as 1,373, and it had 20 ships.

Piracy was rife. Perhaps this is alluded to in the town's motto 'Ad morem villae de Poole' ('according to the custom of the town of Poole') which made its first appearance about this time. A letter of 1582 records that pirates 'cut down the gallows where the pyratt was hanged at Studland; and if reformacon be not had this Somer, no man will be able to travell'. Alive to external dangers a lookout was established at Werybarrow, but trade carried on. Foreign-going vessels were forbidden to sail but the *Primrose* of Poole under the command of 'certain contempteous persons' set sail for Newfoundland. Meanwhile demands for ships for the navy went unheeded.

Poole was pleased with the reign of Elizabeth for in 1568 it obtained from her its greatest charter. The burgesses wished to be free of the interference of Dorset in their affairs and, despite opposition from the manor of Canford, then in the hands of Lord Mountjoy who hoped to exploit alum deposits, it was granted the status of 'one entire county corporate in deed and name distinct and altogether separate from the County of Dorset'. Henceforth it was styled the 'County of the Town of Poole', with the right to appoint its own sheriff. The charter cost £173 12s. 3d. and gave a status shared with London and only 16 other towns and cities in the country. It freed the town from the right of the manor to nominate the mayor, gave the mayor and burgesses control of the markets, the right to appoint a recorder and to establish a Free School.

The new status had to be matched with repair and improvement of the town. Between 1569 and 1572 a new Town Hall in Fish (later Castle) Street, a market house and a prison were built, at merchants' expense. The market house proved inconveniently situated next to the Town Hall and had to be rebuilt elsewhere at a cost of £8. The modern age does not have a monopoly in bad planning!

Where did this wealth come from when other towns were declining? In the new spirit of enterprise Poole merchants developed markets for shipping, independently of London or Bristol merchants. Poole had an advantage with its proximity to and historic links with the Channel Islands. Some of its people, like the de Havilands, had settled in Poole. Beer from Dorset grain was in demand. The consumption of Jersey, Guernsey and Alderney was not itself great, but their trade with the Continent at a time when hostilities prohibited direct trade between Britain and the Continent meant that they acted as a valuable entrepôt for the cloth, horses and beer exported, as well as providing return cargoes of wine, canvas and salt. Poole merchants were thus able to invest in their own town and were well placed to finance the even more rewarding cross-Atlantic trade to the fisheries of the Grand Banks which grew up in the 17th century.

Trade took priority over civic affairs in 1583. Christopher Farewell was fined £30 for neglecting the duties of water bailiff to go on a fishing voyage to Newfoundland. Tiny ships like *Primrose* took out supplies and returned with less sweet-smelling codfish and train (cod-liver) oil to sell to Catholic countries where they picked up other valuable cargoes for the return to their home port. Whereas Catholic countries with whom they were in competition shipped the fish back wet, causing many ships to founder, the Poole trade dried and salted the codfish and brought it across dried in barrels. A typical journey saw vessels leave in the spring and return in the autumn. In 1595 the customs dues collected at Poole amounted to £3,121 11s.; those collected at Bristol amounted to £1,533 11s. 9d. and those at Southampton to £1,478 19s. 3½d.

Poole now needed protection from pirates. Appeals to the Crown went unanswered. Little wonder, therefore, that in the Civil War Poole, unlike the rest of Dorset, sided with Parliament. Its defences were strengthened. On the Quay a vessel was placed with guns trained to cover the ferry-crossing from Hamworthy. A wall and ditch were constructed where the railway now runs, with an embattled town gate of two towers. In the town supporters of the King were ousted. In 1643 the Poole garrison made an important capture of a convoy at Yellowham, near Dorchester, carrying £3,000 from Prince Rupert to Weymouth. Sieges of the town by Royalists were unsuccessful and when trickery was used the Royalists were double-crossed by the governor of Poole garrison, Captain Sydenham. Many cavaliers were killed or taken prisoner. Poole attacked royalist Corfe Castle many times before it fell by treachery after a valiant defence by Lady Bankes. A neglected and unmarked relic of the war survives in the Powder House on Baiter where ammunition was stored. In 1651 Christchurch Castle was demolished and the guns transferred to Poole to strengthen its defences. Of Poole's fortifications nothing remains, as when Charles II was restored in 1660 he ordered the destruction of the defences of towns that had opposed the King's forces.

When the Great Plague raged in London in 1665, the same awful pestilence visited Poole and 118 people died. Charles II, who had fled from his court to Salisbury paid a visit to Poole and was taken to Brownsea and entertained to a banquet in the town. By all accounts it was a pleasant visit and any differences due to the town's stance in the Civil War seem to have been forgotten. The same year George Fox, the founder of the Quakers, came to Poole and 'had a serviceable meeting there amongst the sober people at which William Bayly was convinced'. In later years Quaker families provided many of the town's leading citizens, including the White family, later to own a mansion, 'Beechurst' in the High Street.

By 1667 the attitude of Charles II towards the town had changed as he deprived the town of its charters and was not prepared to listen to its petitions. His brother James restored the charters in 1684. When he was driven from the throne in 1688 the fleet of the invading Prince of Orange could be seen from Constitution Hill as it passed down the Channel on its way to Devonshire. James fled to France and the King of France took his part. Once again the Channel was the scene of war and for a while the French ruled the waves. Admiral Tourville's fleet which ravaged the south coast, landing at Teignmouth, appeared off Poole but did not attack.

The heyday of the Newfoundland trade was the 18th century. In the previous century, after the Great Fire of London, the town had been asked to contribute to rebuilding St Paul's. It rustled up £10 and the note accompanying this said that Poole was very small and poor, 'much decayed by late times of hostility, and the deaths of divers of the chiefest inhabitants, the greater part whereof are mariners, now at Newfoundland and gone to sea ... not to return until March'. It was in the Poole custom then (and perhaps is still) to keep its success secret so that it did not attract a rival. It feared the attention of the Press-Gangs who would take away its seamen. Poole was entirely in the hands of the merchants and in turn they brought Newfoundland and its government under their control. They managed to disguise the importance of the port. A 1698 navy survey reported that the shoals in the harbour were very large and the channels very crooked: 'There are few vessels that will venture into it where they can choose to do otherwise ...'. Times were hard in the surrounding agricultural countryside and the opportunity of a new life abroad was one willingly explored, despite the rigours of the voyage.

The Treaty of Utrecht in 1713 banished French competition and provided conditions encouraging settlement. Merchants ceased to be employers of fishermen or planters. Instead they concentrated on their role as carriers, suppliers of clothes and tackle and purchasers of the end product—fish, oil or sealskins. Since they could set the price of purchase and of later sale in the Mediterranean markets and the supplies had been on credit, the end of the season saw many of the planters in debt, unable to afford a passage home, and obliged to buy further supplies and stay another year. The strong merchant firms included the Whites, Spurriers, Jefferys, Lesters, Jolliffes and, later, Garlands and Slades. The value of the trade can be judged from a report in 1788 that the exports from Poole were valued at £100,000 annually and the fish caught off the Grand Banks by Poole vessels amounted to just under half the total trade. Few could surpass Samuel White who left £200,000 in his will. All invested in fine Georgian mansions built in a bid to outdo each other. In the town a fine new Guildhall was built in 1761.

Smuggling, prevalent on the south coast, did not pass the town by and profited many. Nonetheless petitions to the House of Commons in the 1720s prayed for remedy, referring to 'the great decay of their home manufacture by reason of the great quantity of goods run ...'. Not surprisingly the trade was not abated by strong measures and the presence of revenue officers and cutters.

The population of the town (5,000) depended on the merchants and the trade. Despite constant pleas for government convoys to accompany the fleets Poole merchants opposed the established features of government in Newfoundland, for example courts, fearing a loss in their influence. At the close of the century many other ports transferred their trade to the Virginia or Carolina coasts, but this benefited those remaining who obtained high prices for embargoed goods, trading with Spanish and Portuguese towns blockaded by Napoleon. There was, however, new competition from American vessels. After the defeat of Napoleon the collapse halved the price of cod and led merchants to bankruptcy and the people of the town to ruin.

The manor of Poole, under Sir John Webb, still owned a large part of the land in and around Poole and many disputes arose with the corporation concerning its interests when it tried to muscle in on the success of the trade. Attempts to take in part of the shore of the harbour were defeated, and an attempt to extract tolls from traders entering or leaving the town led to the booth being pulled down. The fourth Sir John Webb went on to try and get Parliament to give permission for him to take in 400 acres of land at Parkstone, but the people resisted and established their right for large tracts of heathland and woodland to remain forever unenclosed. Sir John Webb submitted to the decisions and judgements to cause no trouble; as a Roman Catholic he expected little support from the establishment.

The merchants were rapidly cut down to size in the 19th century with the collapse of the Newfoundland trade and a series of spectacular bankruptcies; the town suffered with them. Any remaining influence they sought to retain was diminished by reform as it robbed them of their right to nominate the town's two members of Parliament and to control the corporation. Reformers challenged as fraudulent the results of the first municipal election for a Poole enlarged by the addition of Hamworthy, Longfleet and Parkstone in 1835 as announced by the Tory mayor. Parliament eventually ordered a fresh election. The lord of the manor went to court over compensation which the old corporation had awarded its former town clerk. While the action continued the magistrates refused to back collection of rates for the corporation to pay the compensation. The former town clerk, Mr. Parr, obtained a court order forcing the Corporation to pay him, but having no assets to pay the town's bills (including those for the newly installed gas lamps) it was obliged to put all the town's possessions in his hands, including the Guildhall and rents from property as well as the maces and Guildhall furniture, which he sold! When the reformers were put in power they dismissed all the officers appointed by the Tories, including the new town clerk, who seized all the documents of the town as a lien for his unpaid bills. Meanwhile Mr. Parr had seized the Guildhall and let it to a farmer for £50 a year. The borough, once the 'Metropolis of Newfoundland' was, like the merchants, reduced to bankruptcy. The final court decision, which awarded Mr. Parr £7,000 compensation and costs, was met only by selling the town's last asset, the right to nominate the rector of St James' church, and taking out a mortgage which lasted to 1865.

In the town's darkest days external developments shaped its future. The Industrial Revolution passed it by, but steam-shipping, a cross-channel ferry and the railway line to Hamworthy arrived on the scene. The hemp industry, which had supported rope walks at Hamworthy, Sterte and Ladies Walking Field, declined as steel came into use for rigging. Markets gave way to shops. The only constant was the export of Purbeck clay, a vital ingredient of Wedgwood and other Staffordshire potteries. The manor of Canford changed hands to the Guest family (later given the title of Lord Wimborne), who initially sought no political sway in Poole and regarded the manor as a useful retreat from their ironworks in the industrial valley at Dowlais. Lady Charlotte was to become involved in many improving schemes, including distinctive cottages with market gardens.

The key to the future of Poole was clay. The bricks and pipes it made, and timber imported from abroad, were in great demand for the building boom then experienced by Bournemouth, which was fast becoming a fashionable health resort. It was not long before the population of Bournemouth outstripped that of Poole. Services were needed by the former village which Poole businesses supplied. At the same time the best parts of Bournemouth were being built in Poole on the Branksome Park Estate.

Confidence deserted the town when county councils were set up in 1888 and it passed over its opportunity to become a county borough. Self-esteem was only restored with a new library, a hospital and a people's park. Poole Pottery was established and an iron works in the Old Town area made steam locomotives. The corporation established a tram route to the Bournemouth boundary at County Gates. Marconi was carrying out his early wireless telegraphy experiments from the *Haven Hotel* and his yacht *Elettra.*

As the 20th century opened the town (population 19,580) was in the shadow of its offspring, Bournemouth. Measures to redress this included the establishment of new schools, overseen by the Carter family of Poole and Kinson potteries. The borough was enlarged in 1905 by the addition of Branksome Urban District and in 1933 by the Poole Rural District, which embraced Broadstone and Canford Magna. Road-building and a new municipal building created work, and the town set its sights on developing a tourist industry of its own. Beach facilities, natural chines and open spaces were all improved, while the use of the harbour for pleasure sailing with the associated boat-building and chandlery businesses was also encouraged. This was also an important period for the arts, with many leading figures in the art and literary world including Stanley Spencer, Henry Lamb and Augustus John being associated with the borough.

The Second World War united the town's efforts and brought its marine skills to the fore. The area also housed important cordite facilities. The town was established as the base of Combined Operations and later the Special Boat Squadron, to play its clandestine part in many operations including the Dieppe Raid, Walcheren, the Falklands War and Gulf War. American forces were deployed in the area prior to the D-Day invasion. Successful decoys on Brownsea Island diverted bombing from the town.

After the war the town resoundingly rejected Abercrombie's plan to join it with Bournemouth and Christchurch, and was spurred on to find new prosperity. Trusting ownership more than planning controls to prevent a 'costa geriatrica', most of South Canford Heath was bought and released for mixed development. A variety of new manufacturing industries, some (like Ryvita and BDH) relocated because of the war, was attracted. Industrial development was not given any special government help, but was achieved by the town itself. Office jobs in insurance and banking were also encouraged. Poole sought county borough status and again opposed talk of a Bournemouth 'takeover'. Slum clearance and new housing ensured that young people, well educated locally, could stay in the area and have a chance of a job. The town had learnt a century earlier the price of reliance on a single source of wealth. Its growth was complemented by new community, leisure and shopping facilities, so that money earned in the area remained within it as long as possible. Public investment in this infrastructure was made from the surplus achieved on land transactions. The results were modern shopping malls, new roads, a new central library, an indoor swimming-pool, a sports centre and one of the largest arts complexes in the country. Bournemouth Orchestras transferred their base to Poole, and Brownsea Island was secured as a natural asset and a shrine to the birthplace of Scouting.

The 1974 reorganisation of local government left the area's boundaries intact, but control over education, libraries, strategic planning and transportation was lost to the county council. Poole was also deprived of its county style, although the offices of sheriff and recorder were retained as honorary titles. Poole was well-placed to withstand recession following the property crash and the oil price hike. Its port was modernised with roll-on roll-off facilities and ferries to France and the Channel Islands. The Higher Education Institute became a polytechnic and then a university. Poole industries have won many Queen's Awards.

The town (now over 136,000 people) has been admired for its dynamism and ability to succeed in its objectives, establishing quality high-technology industries to replace declining activities. Only in very recent years have the recession and peace dividend taken their toll in business closures and contraction hindering consolidation of the borough's success. Oil recovery from beneath the harbour and Poole Bay, while producing large revenues for the Exchequer and being serviced from Poole, has not protected the town. The bright spot is that the long and proud independence of Poole has been recognised by the Local Government Commission recommending that it should become a unitary authority enjoying sole care of Poole's public affairs 'according to the custom of Poole'.

Celebrating Past Events

1 The charter of 1248, measuring only 11½ by 7 inches, is the oldest document in the Borough Archives. The 70 marks paid to William Longespee II for it enabled him to go on a crusade, on which he was killed in 1249. 70 marks was a great deal of money, perhaps £4,000 in today's terms. A building labourer earned 1½d. a day.

2 This carved coat of arms of Poole (1554) was rescued from an old building in 1746 by antiquarian and merchant, Sir Peter Thompson, and re-sited in his mansion in 1779. It is now in Scaplen's Court. 1n 1563 Clarenceux King of Arms confirmed these arms. In 1976 Oscar Murton, M.P. from 1964, gave the town a new grant, incorporating supporters.

3 The fortunes of the town for 200 years lay in the Newfoundland codfish trade. This 1890 photograph of Quidi Vidi shows fish drying and barrowing still being carried out exactly as it would have been in earlier centuries by men of Poole.

4 This fleet of over 60 vessels, pictured at Trinity, Newfoundland, was owned at one time or another by brothers Isaac and Benjamin Lester. In vessels like these, thousands of men and tons of fish and provisions crossed the Atlantic during the 18th century. With the profits the Lesters built the Mansion House in Thames Street.

5 The house on the left was built for Benjamin Lester in Trinity, Newfoundland with bricks and glass transported from Poole *c*.1760. It is the oldest brick-built house in North America and now lies in ruins. Trinity Trust plans to restore it for the Cabot Centenary in 1997. An identical house built for the Lesters at Post Green is now the home of Sir Thomas Lees.

6 Until 1835 the 'Town and County of the Town of Poole's' boundaries were limited to the Old Town. Beyond that area was almost entirely heathland. This aerial photograph from 20 years ago contains the whole 160 acres of the original town. Only in the last 150 years has the built-up area extended beyond the railway line at the top of the picture.

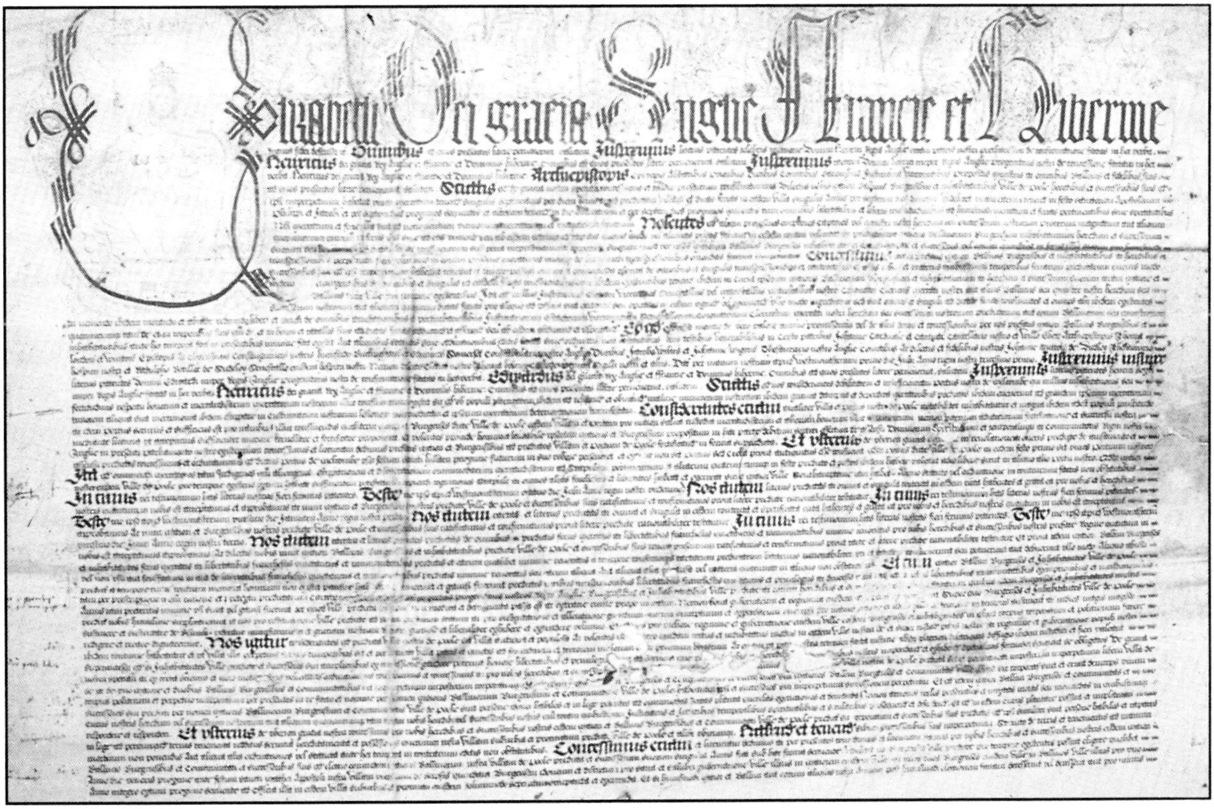

Elizabeth Dei gratia Anglie Francie et Hibernie

7 Petitions seeking a Great Charter (not asking for county status) from a reluctant Queen Elizabeth I began in 1559 and succeeded (with county status) in 1568. Poole's population was only 1,400. The townspeople had to buy the support of Lord of the Manor, Lord Mountjoy. The Queen believed she was confirming earlier grants. Poole was the only county corporate she created.

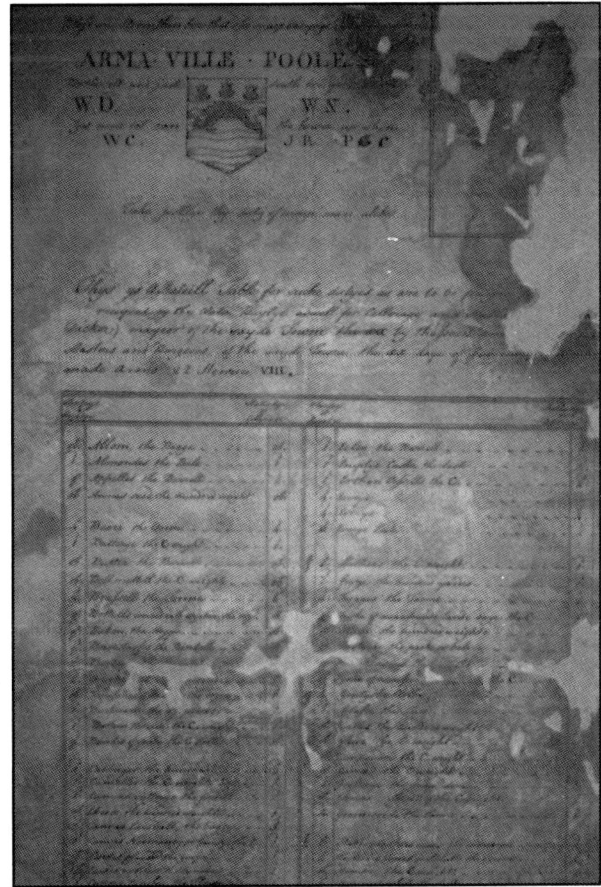

8 The damaged 1579 Ratal specifies the levies on imported goods. The town clerk, John Forrest, added a lot of his own good advice, 'Take justly thy duty of every man alike' and (in Latin) 'When the wise man speaks he awaits the time and the hour/ When the fool speaks he knows, by Hercules, no delay'.

9 In 1747 thirty armed men broke into the Custom House and carried off two tons of impounded tea, valued at £500. The Hawkhurst Gang had 'liberated' what had been seized from them by the Revenue. In escaping to Sussex they committed a murder. Ten men were executed for these offences.

10 Poole Council was a customer of G. W. Ledgard & Sons' Town and County of Poole Bank, founded in 1821. It crashed in 1861 bringing ruin to businesses such as the Slade Newfoundland empire, though it ultimately repaid 85 pence in the pound. Absorbed into Wilts and Dorset Bank and then into Lloyds in 1914, it is still the Council's bank.

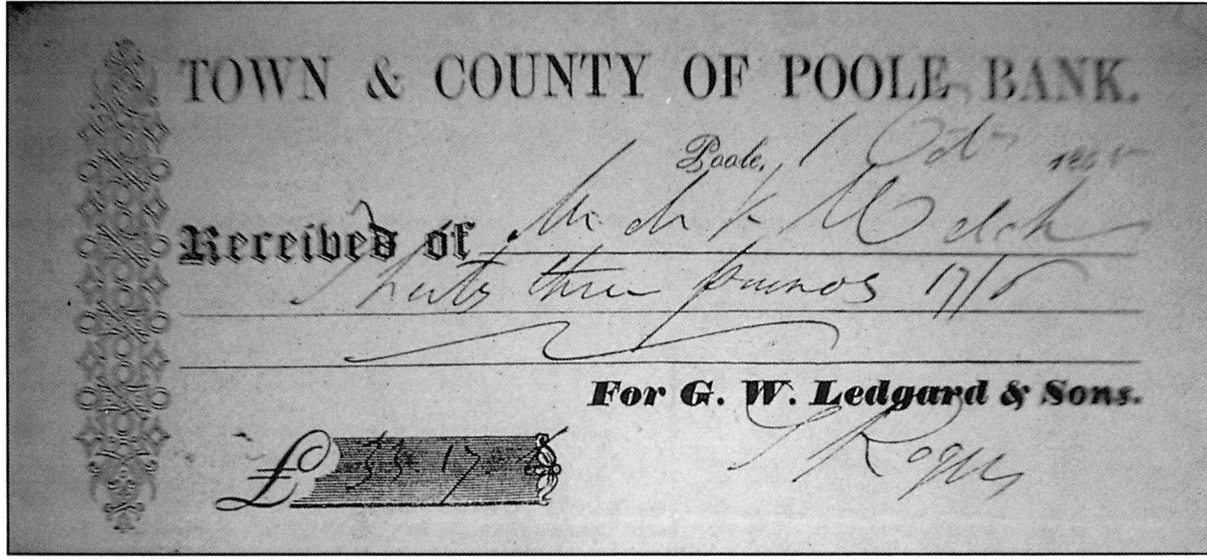

TOWN & COUNTY OF POOLE BANK.

Poole, 1 Oct

Received of

For G. W. Ledgard & Sons.

£

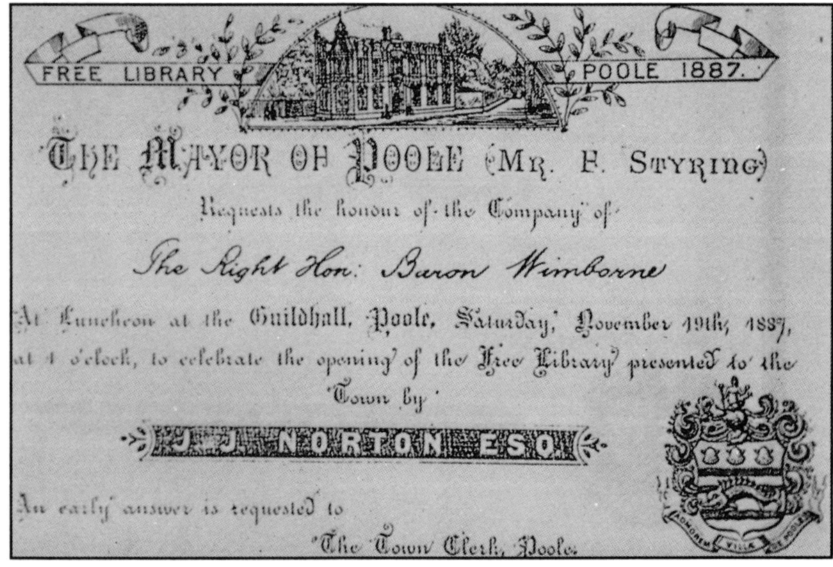

FREE LIBRARY POOLE 1887.

THE MAYOR OF POOLE (MR. F. STYRING)

Requests the honour of the Company of

The Right Hon: Baron Wimborne

At Luncheon at the Guildhall, Poole, Saturday, November 19th, 1887, at 1 o'clock, to celebrate the opening of the Free Library presented to the Town by

J. J. NORTON ESQ.

An early answer is requested to

The Town Clerk, Poole.

11 Lord Wimborne and J. J. Norton offered rival gifts of a hospital and a library to mark Queen Victoria's Golden Jubilee in 1887. The Council selected Norton's library as cheaper to run but had to buy the site from Lord Wimborne. The conveyance took six months. Norton constructed the building in five months, working both day and night using electric lights.

12 In 1975 Poole was selected as one of four demonstration projects in the UK for European Architectural Heritage Year in recognition of the work done to preserve buildings and find new uses for them in the Special Precinct of the Old Town. The design illustrated was used by Poole Pottery for a commemorative plate given to official visitors which marked the honour and recorded the outline of some outstanding buildings.

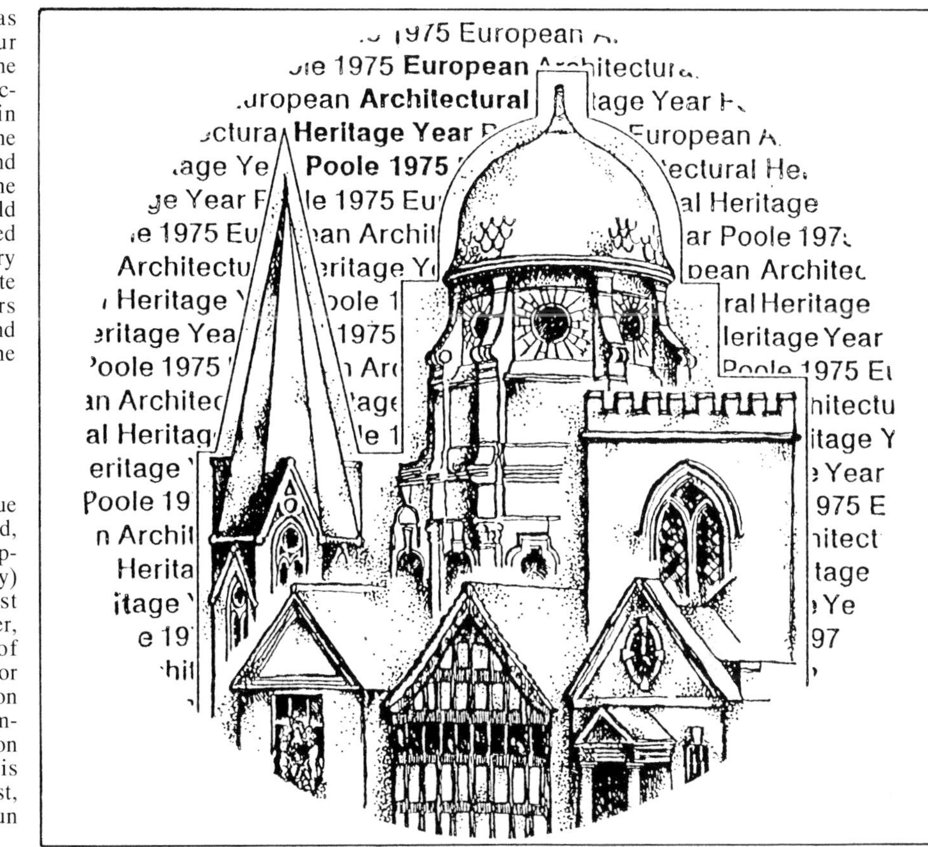

13 This Elliott's royal blue charabanc in Ashley Road, Parkstone is canvassing support in 1906 (unsuccessfully) for Capt. Freddie Guest (Liberal). In 1910 his mother, Lady Cornelia Guest of Canford Manor, canvassed for him and was guilty of election malpractices including intimidating tenants. His election was declared void. His brother, Hon C. H. Guest, replaced him in the re-run election.

14 In the December 1910 General Election Capt. Freddie Guest regained the parliamentary seat which he retained until 1922. He was Chief Whip to Lloyd George and later Secretary of State for Air. A car-borne audience awaits the declaration of the result at the *King's Head Hotel*, Wimborne. Poole was part of East Dorset constituency from 1885 to 1950.

15 A stagecoach was used to convey Ald. Leonard Ballard (mayor), George W. Green (sheriff), and Charles Lisby (appointed as the town's first full-time town clerk in 1907) and the two mace-bearers at the Proclamation of King George V in May 1910. The *London Tavern* in High Street was later rebuilt and called *The Old Harry* after Harry Paye.

16 Poole Park, given by Lord Wimborne, opened in 1890, and to the present day has been a popular venue for Sunday promenades. Band concerts were provided at the expense of the council, £20 a year being allocated for this for many years.

17 The ceremony of 'Beating the Bounds' of Poole's Admiralty jurisdiction was revived in 1921. A jury of 12 men chosen by the Society of Poole Men dress in the naval costumes of Nelson's day.

18 Pirates soon intervened. Certain people not invited to take part by the mayor as 'Admiral of the Port' made a nuisance of themselves. In 1961 a further band of pirates, the charity fund-raising Company and Fellowship of Jolly Pirates, was formed. Once the town's barmaids were abducted and chained to lamp-posts. Here the kidnap of Eric Sykes seems imminent!

19 Sir Winston Churchill was honoured with the freedom of the borough. He opened Parkstone Liberal Club in 1910 and was closely connected with Poole through the Guest family. They also crossed the floor of the House to become Tories in the 1930s. He received the honour in 1954 from Miss Mary Llewellin, the first lady mayor and first honorary Alderman.

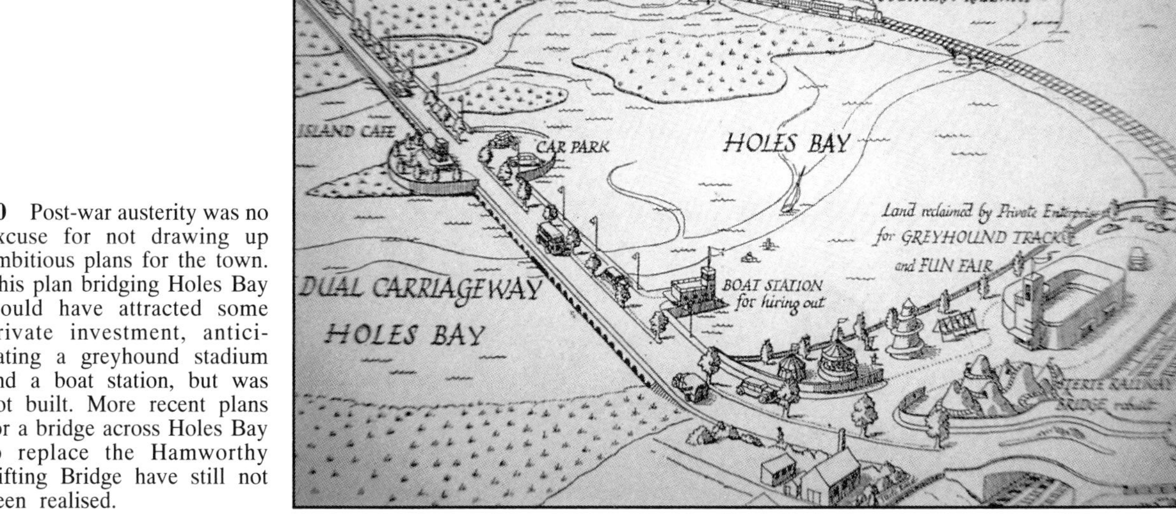

20 Post-war austerity was no excuse for not drawing up ambitious plans for the town. This plan bridging Holes Bay would have attracted some private investment, anticipating a greyhound stadium and a boat station, but was not built. More recent plans for a bridge across Holes Bay to replace the Hamworthy Lifting Bridge have still not been realised.

TWINNING OF POOLE AND CHERBOURG

Declaration of Friendship between POOLE and CHERBOURG

At a ceremony held this day, 24th September, 1977, at Poole, the Town of Cherbourg represented by its Mayor, Louis Darinot, and Poole by its Mayor, John Malcolm Norman, and its Town Clerk and Chief Executive Officer, Ian Keith David Andrews, ratified their decision to link with one another and to initiate linguistic, tourist, economic and social exchanges for the mutual benefit of all the people of their towns.

The twinned Towns hope that this union opens the way to a greater understanding between the citizens of France and Great Britain, as well as between those of all other nations.

The Seal of the Council of the Borough of Poole was hereunto affixed in the presence of:

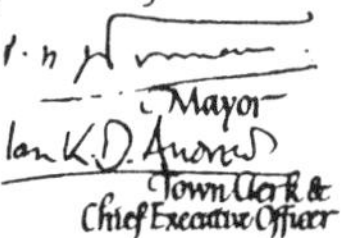

Mayor

Town Clerk & Chief Executive Officer

In witness of which the Seal of the Town of Cherbourg was affixed in the presence of:

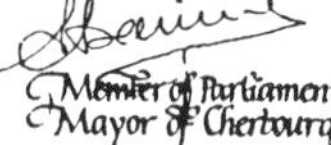

Member of Parliament Mayor of Cherbourg

JUMELAGE CHERBOURG-POOLE

Protocole d'amitie entre CHERBOURG et POOLE

Au cours d'une réunion tenue aujourd'hui 24 septembre 1977 à Poole, la ville de Cherbourg, représentée par son Maire, Louis Darinot ; et la ville de Poole, representee par son Maire, John Malcolm Norman, et par son Chef du Secrétariat, Ian Keith David Andrews, ont confirmé leur résolution de s'associer et de procéder à des échanges linguistiques, touristiques, économiques et sociaux interessant l'ensemble de leur population.

Les deux villes-jumelles souhaitent que cette union ouvre la voie à une meilleure compréhension entre les citoyens de France et de Grande-Bretagne, ainsi qu'entre ceux de toutes les autres nations.

En foi de quoi le sceau de la Ville de Cherbourg fut apposé sur ce parchemin en présence de

Député-Maire de Cherbourg

En foi de quoi le sceau du Conseil Municipal de Poole fut apposé sur ce parchemin en présence de

Maire de Poole

Chef du Secrétariat

21 In 1977 Poole became twinned officially with Cherbourg, which at 60 miles is nearer to the port than London. Relations with the French had their ups and downs in earlier centuries. In 1830 the ex-King Charles X of France and his retinue had made their escape from France to Hamworthy.

22 The author, as Chairman of Poole Arts Trust, wearing his town clerk's wig and gown, meets the Princess of Wales and introduces trustees on a royal visit in 1988. The Centre was opened in 1978 and received a visit from H.M. The Queen and Prince Philip in 1979. The centre, one of the largest in the country, cost five million pounds and is now valued at over 30 million pounds.

Civic Offices

Thicky Burrer Council ... they mos'ly tries to do their best, zum o'm talks mor'n they doos and zum o'm doos mor'n they talks. I doan' know as 'ow I'd 'ave the heart to call any of o'm vools, neet rogues, praps they be a bit of a mixture, seame's me an' you.' (Alderman Herbert Carter).

23 The first town seal of La Pole dates from the early 14th century. Where early meetings were held is not clear, but may include 'the towne house' mentioned in the early records of the town, which date from 1490.

24 The 1761 Guildhall replaced an Elizabethan building in Fish Street (Castle Street) with a prison beneath it. A plaque records it as a gift from Gulston and Calcraft, the town's two MPs; in fact the Council raised a mortgage to pay for it. Income was obtained from the open arcaded market beneath the Council Chamber.

25 As the town grew it needed municipal offices as well as a meeting place. Sir Peter Thompson's 1752 mansion in Pillory (now Market) Street, designed by John Bastard, was purchased by the Council in 1907 and used until 1932. Earlier owners had included Frederick Styring of Poole Brewery and Sir Ivor Guest (Lord Wimborne), who founded Cornelia Hospital.

26 In the 1890s Branksome UDC was courted by both Bournemouth and Poole, but resisted amalgamation, defiantly erecting its own Council Building in Shillito Road in 1901. In 1905 Poole Borough took over. For many years a highway depot, in 1962 it was used for test broadcasts for BBC 'local' radio. In 1984 it was the set for 'Miss Marple'.

27 These trams at Sloop Hill in 1908 are running past the site (right) of the future Municipal Buildings at Brown Bottom, Park Gates East. Controversy and opposition met the proposal to move 'off centre' from the Old Town. Fernside Road was then known as Breakheart Lane. The tram shelter was later used at Fisherman's Hard.

28 The area of the borough was enlarged to include Broadstone and Canford Magna in 1933, making the borough population 53,000. By a 21 to 13 vote new offices had been commissioned in 1931. A hundred men worked for Whitelock and Co. for 62 weeks to complete the Municipal Building at a cost of £62,290. 900,000 bricks were laid.

29 Borough Surveyor, E. J. Goodacre, is named on the foundation-stone, but the distinguished design was by his assistant, L. Magnus Austin, who obtained his own credit by incorporating his monogram in the seaweed decorating the keystone above the members' entrance!

30 The building contains many decorative details. A walk round the exterior tells the story of Poole. 24 bas-reliefs of events in Poole's history were commissioned at three guineas each from Eustace Nash, but Percival A. Wise, the Head of the Art School, offered to do the job at a third of the price and was awarded the contract!

31 In planning for post-war expansion it was realised that an enlarged Civic Centre would be needed. This 1958 model of possible new buildings (not implemented) at the Civic Centre included a swimming pool and civic hall for entertainment. Instead an award winning health clinic, law courts and an undistinguished crown building emerged.

'The Town Clerk, Surveyor, Accountant, Police
Are all of them ready the poor public to fleece
And 'gainst all good reason they insist, they demand
That we build a Town Hall on the Park Gates East land'
quipped Alderman Herbert Carter.

Public Services

32 Poole pioneered gasworks, starting in 1833. Most of the plant pictured at Pitwines had been built in 1924. Its demolition created problems when the retort house refused to yield to explosives, but care had to be taken because of the nearby railway.

33 An aerial cableway brought coal from the quay. Dust from the coal caused a great nuisance to nearby homes. The Grammar School lay across the railway line. One wit wrote, 'Up to yon massive gassy plant/Our border doth abide/And we must thank our sainted aunt/It doesn't come inside.'

TO THE

INHABITANTS

OF THE

TOWN AND COUNTY OF POOLE.

It is to be feared from the reports contained in the Public Papers, that the Cholera Morbus, which has proved so fatal in Asia and various parts of Europe, has made its appearance in England. It becomes, therefore, the Duty of every one to exert himself to prevent, if possible, the introduction of this direful Disease into his own Family, Town, or Neighbourhood.

By Order of Government, a BOARD OF HEALTH has been formed in this Town, consisting of the Magistrates, the Sheriff, the Parochial Minister, the Collector and Comptroller of the Customs, and the Gentlemen of the Medical Profession; who will at all times be ready to afford any information, or receive any communication that may tend to promote the Health of the Inhabitants.

The Board of Health have endeavoured to obtain the best information as to the most effectual means of Preventing the Introduction or Spread of this Disease, and they beg to call the attention of their fellow Townsmen to a few suggestions which they earnestly beseech them to adopt, believing that if they do so, they will prove efficacious (under the divine blessing) in preventing the introduction or spread of the Cholera Morbus in Poole.

First. The Board recommend constant attention to EXTERNAL CLEANLINESS. That the Streets, Lanes, and other Highways of the Town, be kept free from Dirt, Filth, or Stagnant Water; and they hope that every Householder will cheerfully co-operate with the Scavengers in endeavoring to accomplish this important object; and as there are but few public Pumps, that they will cause a few Buckets of Water to be daily thrown into the Gutter opposite their respective Dwellings, in order to prevent Noxious Exhalations arising therefrom, which are at all times very prejudicial to health.

Second. The Board recommend INTERNAL CLEANLINESS. That no accumulation of Dirt, or Decayed Vegetables or Fruit, be allowed to remain in or about their Habitations, but that every care be taken to keep their Houses Clean and well Ventilated. A free circulation of Air is of much importance, the Windows should therefore be opened as often as Weather will permit.

Third. PERSONAL CLEANLINESS. It is very important that Parents should pay particular attention to their Children being kept clean, and sufficiently Clothed to protect them from the Effects of Cold and Damp Weather, and those who from extreme Poverty are unable to do so, should make known their situation to their Wealthier Neighbours, whose liberality they may be assured will be manifested as on all former occasions.

Fourth. The Board earnestly recommend a strict regard to Habits of Temperance and Sobriety, as nothing tends to predispose the human frame to disease, more than intemperance. *All immoderate use of Spirituous Liquors should especially be avoided.*

Fifth. The Board desire to impress on the Inhabitants, the great importance of the earliest possible application to Medical Aid, should any person be attacked by any disease that may resemble the Cholera Morbus. This is a matter of much moment, and cannot be too powerfully urged on the attention of all classes, as the progress of this disease is generally so rapid, that it is only by an early application of Medical Skill that beneficial results can at all be relied on. *That the Poor may be encouraged so to do, the Medical Gentlemen have kindly promised their services to them gratuitously.*

Lastly. While the Board have felt it their duty to place these Remarks before the Inhabitants by way of Caution and Guidance, they feel pleasure in encouraging them to hope and believe that such is the Climate of England, that if general attention be paid to Cleanliness, Ventilation, and Sobriety, together with timely application for Medical advice and assistance, the continuance of this Disease in England will not be long, but that our Country will speedily, by the blessing of God, be freed from its direful consequences. All unnecessary Fear and Anxiety should therefore, be avoided, under the full assurance that if we invoke the Protection of an invisible but Almighty Guardian, and diligently use the appointed means of safety, he will crown our endeavours with his blessing.

ON BEHALF OF THE BOARD,

G. W. LEDGARD, ***Mayor,***

CHAIRMAN.

34 An outbreak of cholera caused this set of rules to be circulated in 1831. Panic and strong liquor were to be avoided and doctors gave their services free to poor patients. A Society for Relief of the Sick and Aged had been formed in 1815, with subscriptions of 4d. a month, but the town had no hospital.

To the Inhabitants

OF THE

TOWN AND COUNTY OF POOLE.

The Surveyors of the Highways, anxious at all times to perform the duties which devolve upon them, according to the best of their abilities and the means placed at their disposal, feel, at the present Juncture, a peculiar solicitude that nothing should be omitted on their part, that can keep the Town in a state of cleanliness and thereby preserve the health of the people; They therefore take the liberty to call the attention of the inhabitants to *the condition of the gutters,* which in consequence of the level state of the Streets, can only be kept clean and wholesome by a plentiful supply of water. *They therefore respectfully, but earnestly request that every householder will cause six buckets of water (at the least) to be thrown into the gutter opposite his house, every morning* AT NINE O'CLOCK.

JAMES SALTER,
TITO D. HODGES. } *Surveyors.*

POOLE, July 24th, 1832.

LANKESTER, PRINTER, POOLE.

35 By 1832 the causes of cholera were understood and practical measures were taken to get each household to throw six buckets of water in the town's filthy gutters at precisely 9 o'clock each morning. In 1829 a Poole surgeon, named Mr. Timewell, met the town's MPs seeking support for a hospital, but the timing was not auspicious.

36 Charles William Packe built Branksome Tower (pictured), designed by William Burn, in 1854 and owned the private 745-acre estate approached via Packe (now known as County) Gates in Poole. He set up a public dispensary in Bournemouth in 1859 which provided the only facilities for Poole, Bournemouth and Christchurch residents and he planned a hospital at Westbourne.

37 Not until 1888 was a hospital available in Poole, when Lord and Lady Wimborne made a gift of West Street premises. Later moved to Weston House, and temporarily to Sir Peter Thompson's mansion, in 1907 Cornelia Hospital settled into these purpose-built premises in Longfleet Road.

BOROUGH OF POOLE

WARNING.

I am instructed by the Town Council to again issue a Warning to the Inhabitants of the Borough of the danger of contracting Typhoid Fever, Diarrhœa, &c., through the eating of UNCOOKED Shell-fish (Oysters, Mussels, Cockles, etc.)

Cockles, Mussels and Oysters should have their shells firmly closed when taken out of water, and if in water the open shell should close when touched. When a marked proportion of the shells show a tendency to gape, and the shells of others are easily separated, the batch should be considered as unsound and unfit for food.

In any case before opening, the shells should be thoroughly scrubbed with a stiff brush and rinsed in clean water.

G. H. CARRINGTON, D.P.H.,

September 16th, 1907. *Medical Officer of Health.*

38 After typhoid was reported, Poole Council diverted sewage from Hamworthy Battery Barracks in 1902, but cases continued and suspicion fell on casual hawkers of oysters. In 1907 advice, still good today, was promulgated. In 1936 another outbreak (18 people died) was traced to milk from cows grazing in contaminated water at Merley.

39 In the early days the Fire Brigade engine was often not able to reach outlying districts until it was too late. At some fires the hoses were too short. By the early 1900s the brigade was able to display in Poole Park modern two-in-hand and steam equipment. The first motor vehicle was purchased in 1928.

40 Changes in Poole Fire Brigade helmets are being demonstrated. The issue of uniforms was the subject of debate in 1884. Some thought a conspicuous badge and helmet were all that was required, as putting on 'fine clothes' would delay departure. Poole Fire Brigade merged into the National Fire Service in 1941.

41 Bournemouth and Poole Electricity Supply Co. Ltd. used handcarts to convey equipment and the once familiar tents to protect their exposed underground service. Mr. Henson, one of their employees, is in the front of this picture. In some parts of the borough, electricity is still supplied by overhead line.

aſſembled; and ſhall, in their ſeveral Turns or Courſes of watching, uſe their beſt Endeavours to prevent as well all Miſchiefs happening by Fire, as all Murders, Burglaries, and other Diſorders; and to that end ſhall arreſt and apprehend all Malefactors, and ſuſpected or diſorderly Perſons, who ſhall be found wandering or misbehaving themſelves; and ſhall carry the Perſons, who ſhall be ſo apprehended, as ſoon as conveniently may be, before the ſaid Mayor, or One of the Juſtices of the Peace, for the ſaid Town and County of the ſaid Town, to be examined and dealt with according to Law; and ſhall twice, or oftener, at convenient Times in every Night, go about their reſpective Wards, Diſtricts, Precincts, or Stations, and take

endeavour to prevent Miſchiefs by Fire,

apprehend diſorderly Perſons,

42 In 1756 Poole Harbour Act authorised a 'watch and ward' of the town, a precursor of 'neighbourhood watch' with a view to apprehending murderers and burglars. The same Act prohibited the keeping of more than 10lb. of explosive in the town and set up a powder-house at Baiter.

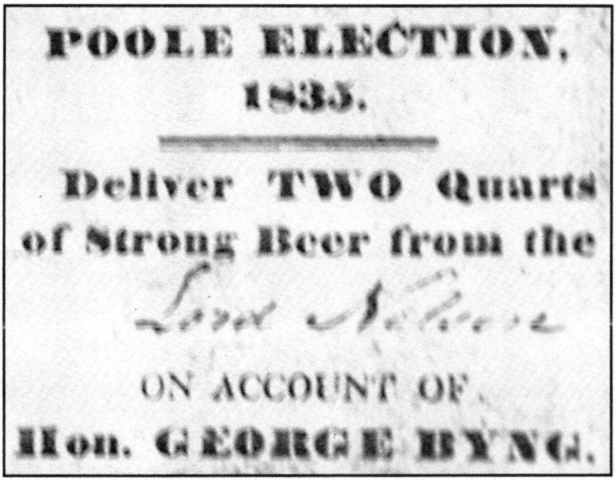

POOLE ELECTION,
1835.

Deliver TWO Quarts
of Strong Beer from the
Lord Nelson
ON ACCOUNT OF
Hon. GEORGE BYNG.

43 Election times were always riotous in Poole. The vote was restricted to burgesses but in 1835 the franchise was extended. One way of ensuring votes was to give away beer in return for a favour, as this beer ticket shows. Law and order were hard to maintain. What was needed was a police force.

44 The borough police force was formed in 1836, consisting of 21 constables, and a superintendent. Plans (above) were drawn up for police headquarters next to the Guildhall. In 1839 a 1s. pay rise to 14s. a week was ordered to keep wages above those of tradesmen and assure police independence.

45 The ratio of one constable to 400 people was more generous than the Metropolitan Police and was expensive. When Liberals won control of the borough in 1841 they reduced numbers to nine constables. Crimes included 'driving a cart drawn by dogs' in 1853 and 'throwing snowballs' in 1858. Newfoundland dogs (as below) were prized, but from 1841 were not allowed to draw carts.

To M. SEAGER, Esq.

HIGH SHERIFF OF THE TOWN AND COUNTY OF THE TOWN OF POOLE.

Poole, June 24, 1829.

Sir,

We request that you will please to convene a MEETING of the INHABITANTS of this Town, to take into consideration the intended discontinuance of the MAIL COACH, and adopt such measures as may appear best on the occasion.

We are, Sir,
Yours very respectfully,

PETER JOLLIFF
T. JOYCE
WM. B. BEST
W. JOLLIFFE, Mayor.
J. BRISTOWE, & Co.
JAS. SEAGER.
C. SPURRIER & Co.
HARRISON, SLADE, & Co.
FRYER, ANDREWS, & Co.
SALTER, BALSTON, & Co.
THOMAS GADEN
GADEN & ADEY

June 25th, 1829.

In compliance with the above Requisition; I appoint a MEETING of the Inhabitants of this Town and County, to be holden

At the GUILDHALL,

On Monday next,

AT ELEVEN O'CLOCK.

M. SEAGER, Sheriff.

46 In 1829 the town's decline led to the threatened withdrawal of its mail coach to London. The sheriff exercised one of his rights, to call a town meeting, as this poster reveals. The last sheriff's meeting was held in the 1960s to protest at possible encroachment on Poole Park by highways.

Wartime

47 Volunteers shown under canvas in the early part of the century—perhaps after the Boer War, judging by what appears to be a Zulu spear.

48 Three ships have borne the name HMS *Poole*. The first, a 32-gunner, was built in Cowes in 1696 and was sunk in 1737 as part of the foundations of Harwich Harbour. In 1745 another 5th rate HMS Poole was built in Hull and broken up in 1765. The last HMS *Poole*, pictured at Poole, was a Bangor Class minesweeper of 650 tons, launched in 1941. By 1943 her stokers were writing to the Mayor seeking pen pals and pin-up photos. HMS Poole was broken up in 1948, having given good service in the invasions of Madagascar, Sicily and Normandy.

49 In 1939 the *Poole and East Dorset Herald* pronounced that 'War found Poole Calm and Ready'. Against a background of advertisements for Poole Investment Bank, Amity Cinema and Players' cigarettes, the Dorset British Legion held a well-attended rally.

50 The town subscribed towards a Spitfire, pictured above. 'Villae de Poole' was built in February 1941 at Woolston as a Mk I, but was adapted as a Mark V. It served only briefly with a training unit before it crashed near Chester in December 1941 during a snowstorm.

51 In 1940, 3,000 refugees fled in small ships to Poole from Holland and Belgium as the Germans advanced. They moored in Brownsea Roads, seen in this water-colour painting by P. Sharpe, and were shepherded to temporary accommodation on Brownsea Island for medical and other checks before being allowed on the mainland.

52 Poole Auxiliary Fire Service demonstrate their method of overcoming the Fuehrer.

53 The town suffered comparatively little from bombing and displayed its indignation and defiance when it did occur.

54 Poole Bridge sketched by Leading Seaman Lucas. It proved a headache for the authorities, lest it be bombed, as important repair facilities and berths lay above the bridge. It was also difficult to negotiate when towing landing-craft. Had it been bombed and then replaced, many of today's problems would have been solved!

55 A difficult recovery task for Lt. Commander Vandy, in charge of the harbour and moorings during the war. Brownsea Castle is in the background. The craft, manned by fishermen, were the *Gondoliers* and *Skylarks*, built by the local firm of Bolsons which had conveyed visitors on holiday trips before the war. Bolsons were by then busy constructing landing-craft.

56 Photographs of wartime social life, such as this group in the *Port Mahon Hotel* bar, are rare, as the use of photographic film was restricted for private individuals. The notice above the bar reads 'Ladies are requested not to stand at the counter drinking'.

57 Ladies had their place at the pubs. 'Make do and mend' and sewing socks for sailors were part of the stock in trade of the 'Stitch by Stitch' Club at the *Port Mahon*.

58 The Town Quay and vessels in the harbour were protected by barrage balloons. This one was photographed from a minesweeper anchored opposite the *Portsmouth Hoy*. US troops, preparing for D-Day, filled the town and included the first coloured men many locals had seen. US Coastguard Cutters played a valuable role in rescues.

59 US troops embark for the D-Day invasion in June 1944. Many had been billeted in the town, and having been received with kindness repaid townspeople with gifts of food, Hershey bars, gum and cigarettes. The official US records also state 'the finest...and best spirit of co-operation prevailed' in the joint operations with the British Army and Royal Navy.

60 Mayor Joe Bright, a local baker, who had served in that office through the war, sits at the centre of this commemorative picture of the wartime council taken on V.E. Day, 8 May 1945.

Leisure

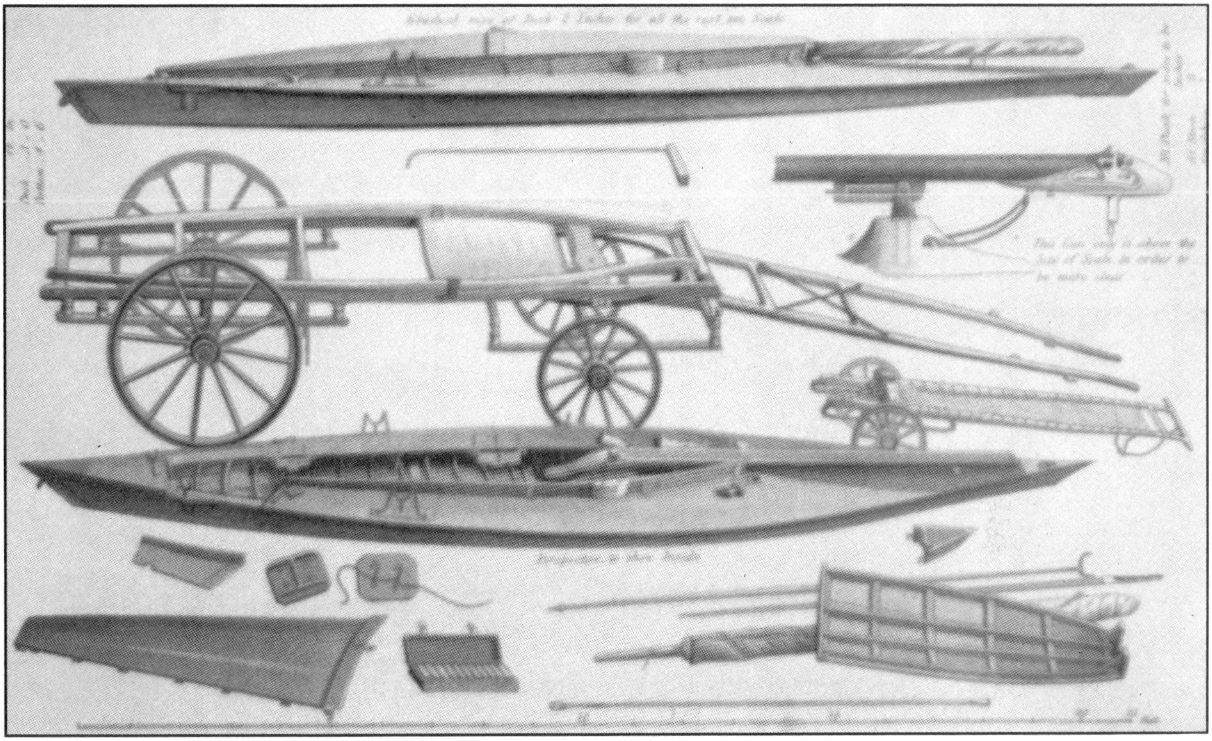

61 Col. Peter Hawker frequented Poole harbour for wildfowling and extolled the virtues of the Poole Canoe, illustrated here. James Reade of Poole, his companion 'the Mozart of all the wild-fowlmen', bagged 44 wigeon in one night in Poole harbour. South Haven was described as a 'paradise for shooters'.

62 Punt Guns of the type Col. Hawker would have known in the early 1800s are displayed at Trinity Museum, Newfoundland. Many of them bear the marks of Poole owners including the Slade and Garland families.

63 Poole Wheelers are a long established local cycling club which has produced many champions. Apart from road racing they also used a specially built cycle track in Poole Park. The photograph shows a local visitor (unfortunately not identified) in the annual sports sometime between 1905-10, with his brakeless racing machine and perhaps his father (or his personal trainer) and his trophies.

64 One of the spring pastimes was to go 'primrosing'. This fashionable group of young ladies and their beaux are pictured at Corfe Mullen, *c.*1900. Each is carrying or wearing a bunch of the wild flowers they had picked and many would have pressed them in scrapbooks on their return.

65 Seats similar to those shown in this Victorian sketch were installed during the 1990 centenary celebration of the gift to the town by Lord Wimborne of land stranded by railway construction. The People's Park was created to prize-winning plans by Borough Surveyor, John Elford, although he had thought the soil unsuitable.

66 Lord Wimborne's own amusement at Canford in 1890 was musical. This photograph shows a banjo and mandolin band, but Italian bands and military music featured as well.

67 By 1914 trees in Poole Park, including horse chestnuts, were well established, but motor traffic was becoming a problem. Boating on Sundays was not allowed on the salt-water lake. A miniature train was introduced in the 1930s as were an aviary, monkey house and, after the War, a zoo. The eagles at the entrance gates originally cost five guineas each.

68 Poole quay has so many public houses it is hard to think of people taking their refreshment elsewhere, but the *Willett Arms* at Merley offered a jaunt into the countryside. The roof is a mixture of thatch and tile. Ralph Willett was a rich sugar plantation owner who built Merley House.

69 At the Haven a pier had been built in 1898 from which a ferry ran to Shell Bay and boats could be hired. In the grounds of *Haven Hotel* is the array of wires used by a Signor Marconi for his experiments in radio communication to his yacht *Elettra* and for his first communication with the Isle of Wight in 1896.

70 Many postcards show the panorama from Constitution Hill, which has been enjoyed by royalty and described as having no rival. This photograph dates from the turn of the century and was taken on a clear day. When Gladstone visited he saw only dreary mudland.

71 Parkstone Park (pictured in 1906) and Poole Park both opened in 1890 to great rejoicing. The *Daily Telegraph* reported, 'The spirit of the old Elizabethan port, once mightier than Southampton, had been aroused, and the ancient town and county—she is a stickler for this title—means to be second to none'.

72 The fountain in Parkstone Park has been replaced, but with nothing like this fine Victorian original. Three Acre Field was acquired from Lord Wimborne as part of complex negotiations for a number of sites involving the exchange of lands at Heatherlands and payment of £400 an acre.

73 The town's first swimming pool in 1890 was open air and tidal. The remains at East Quay are fast disappearing into oblivion as municipal improvements take place. The 1930s saw new swimming baths (above), with changing accommodation, at Kingland Road. The site is now a windsurfing school. The long-awaited heated indoor Central Swimming Pool (Dolphin) opened in 1974.

74 Before the motor car became a universal means of travel, a fortnight's holiday by rail, with passengers' luggage sent in advance, was the dream of many. Southern Railway promoted this with a 1947 poster for Branksome Dene, near the prestigious five-star *Branksome Tower Hotel,* boasting a private beach, which was conveyed to the Council when the site was redeveloped.

75 Before Poole realised it was a beautiful place, a tearoom catered for visitors to Branksome Chine in 1908. The Cabin could provide lobster teas, and in the winter it was used by fishermen who worked their boats from the shore. In earlier centuries smugglers are believed to have run their goods ashore, along the chine and over the Great Heath.

MOTORS
PARK HERE
UB 5715

76 In 1932 the Council bid for high tourism stakes, building a Solarium equipped to supply 'health-giving electric beams of the artificial sun'. Unfortunately the cost of running the ultra-violet lamps (danger then unknown) was higher than expected. The public preferred a nice cup of tea and a cake. Note the care taken to protect cars from the sun.

77 'Keep young and beautiful, if you want to be loved.' The Solarium's contribution to health and beauty (and the modesty of the bathing apparel) are apparent in this 1933 snapshot. Forty years later the Council re-entered the same market, installing a sauna and sunbeds at Dolphin Pool.

78 Land acquired by the Council in 1923 was first used for fairs and a stable-cum-depot for the Council's horse-drawn refuse fleet. This 1930s photograph shows Poole Sports Arena before the erection of the stands and the arrival of speedway.

79 The first speedway meeting was on 26 April 1948, attended by Mayor A. J. Langridge, known as 'Sudan Sam'. The Poole Pirates team owes its existence to Clifford Brewer (left), seen with team members in their distinctive skull and crossbone colours. Captain Charlie Hayden is seated on his machine.

80 The Arts Centre, opened in 1978 and visited by the Queen and Prince Philip in 1979 and the Princess of Wales in 1988, is far too modern to include in this book, but many people ask what was on the site before it was built. In 1865 this terrace known as Kingland Place (demolished 1974) stood at the back on the site.

We Lived Here

81 John Masters (*c*.1688-1755), right, was born in Silly Cove, Newfoundland (now renamed Winterton), came to England in 1697 and was educated in Wimborne. He rose to be a merchant and was twice mayor of Poole, in 1748 and 1752. He aspired to be an MP, but Poole was not ready for 'Newfoundland Monarchy'.

82 George Garland (1753-1825), below left, MP for Poole from 1801 to 1806 and twice mayor, inherited the Newfoundland business of the Lesters. He gave almshouses at Hunger Hill to the town which were demolished for road improvements. His son, John Bingley Garland, also a mayor of Poole, became first Speaker of the Newfoundland House of Assembly in 1832 and gave Poole a new cemetery.

83 Alfred Wallace (1823-1913), below right, retired to Parkstone until it became developed and later lived at Broadstone, where he conducted seances with Conan Doyle. In 1858 he put forward the theory of natural selection, which is popularly attributed to his friend Darwin, who wrote, 'You never demand justice'. He also prophesied 'nuclear power'.

84 'Springfield' in Parkstone was the home of William Pearce, proprietor of the successful Dorset Ironfoundry set up at Baiter Green on the site of a former ropewalk in 1841. The firm originally made agricultural implements and exhibited at the Great Exhibition in 1851. Only the lodge in Bournemouth Road remains of the house which served as Danecourt school until the 1960s.

85 Rev. Peter Jolliffe of Sterte House was vicar of St James' for an astounding 70 years from 1791 until his death in 1861. Evangelical by faith, he nonetheless attended the consecration of the R.C. Church and sent wine for communion when theirs ran out. In 1694 an ancestor had been awarded a royal medal for rescuing a Weymouth ship from privateers.

86 A neighbour of Herbert Carter in Parkstone Heights was Dr. Horace Dobell, whose 1892 house is pictured. In 1886 he published *Bournemouth and Its Surroundings (Its Medical Aspects)* which played a great part in encouraging residence in the area. An influenza victim himself, he acquired 'the most lovely building site in England' and designed this single-storey house 300 feet above sea level.

87 Canon W. Okes Parish was beloved of the congregation of St Mary's, Longfleet. When after 45 years he retired in 1929, he was presented with a car, but said 'I can't drive a car and don't suppose I ever shall'. As Archdeacon of Dorset, he was driven round the diocese by one of his daughters.

88 Louie Dingwall (Miss Foott) (1893-1982) drove ambulances in the First World War, trained racehorses at Sandbanks and was the first woman trainer licensed by the Jockey Club. She ran a bus service (dubbed 'Monkey's Hump and Heavenly Bottom Express') in Rossmore, against all opposition.

89 Harry Peace Smith, MBE (1892-1952) is synonymous with the study of Poole history. Born in Leicestershire, he came to Poole as an uncertificated teacher in 1910 and rose to headmasterships of South Road and Henry Harbin Schools. He published only the first two volumes of a proposed complete history of Poole before he died.

90 In 1964 the town fêted Ann Sidney, the daughter of a local hairdresser and a popular 'Miss Poole', on her selection as 'Miss World'. Mayor Tom Sherrin and Sheriff Adrian Greenwood are seen escorting her to a civic luncheon in Lord Montagu's Silver Cloud. In 1983 another Poole girl, Sarah Jane Hutt, also won the 'Miss World' title.

Shopping

91 Poole acquired market rights in a 1239 charter and was a port of the staple. It had separate sites for fish, green, corn and meat markets. Fish had to be exposed for one hour for locals to buy before foreigners. The Fish Shambles were on the quay. A later market, shown, was let by the Council to Dibbens from 1938-57.

92 Wilts & Dorset Bank on the corner of Albert Road and Ashley Road has changed little since 1906, except to display the name of Lloyds as its successor, but the ornate tram poles cum gas standards have been replaced.

93 Every picture tells a story. This is the shopfront of Caleb Tom Snook's stationery shop in The Broadway, Ashley Road. Finding it in researching this book alone justifies the publication, for closer examination reveals the photograph was taken as news of San Francisco's earthquake hit the news boards after 19 April 1906!

94 By the middle of the 20th century the growth of traffic stifled shopping in the narrow streets of the old town, and the level crossing gates further interrupted life. This part of High Street, by the *Ansty Arms*, now lies under Falkland Square.

95 Co-op Drapery Store in Ashley Road, pictured in the early 1930s. St John's church (with bellcote), was built in 1902-3 at a cost of £5,260, replacing an 1881 building which became the church hall. The tram service started in 1901 and operated until 1935. A constant complaint was of traffic jams behind trams waiting to pass on the loop at Albert Road.

96 The gaslit Beehive Clothing Store of David Phillips was in Ashley Road, near Tennyson Road. This high-class establishment displayed bowler hats, collars, scarves, gloves and rugby suits (10s. 6d., 12s. 6d. and 15s. each) in the window in 1906. Trousers bear price tags of 6s. 11d., 8s. 11d. and 10s. 6d. a pair.

97 Many of the shops in Ashley Road were originally built as houses. The Log Cabin, shoe repairers, pictured in 1906, was one of these.

98 The original façade of Branksome and Upper Parkstone Conservative Club, built in 1888, the site of which was given by Lord Wimborne, its first president. An 'old iron room' in Victoria Road had been its original home. In 1903 the AGM resolved overwhelmingly 'not to entertain the proposal to sell liquor'.

99 The south side of Ashley Road in 1906 shows the corner of the Conservative Club. The parade was occupied by Forseys, the photographer (some of whose photographs are in this book), Churchouse, hairdresser and tobacconist, Hebditch, fruiterer, and Field's Garage, advertised as 'Cycle Agent and General Mechanic'. In 1908 a bicycle cost £3 17s. 6d.

100 The premises of Eastman's, butchers, pictured in 1906, were next door to the Parkstone Empire, Ashley Road, a cinema owned by the Popular Bioscope Syndicate Ltd., which continued in use to 1921. The premises are now Windsers and the former cinema at the rear can be seen from the road.

101 Today's Bournemouth Road is recognisable from this 1905 photograph, including St Osmund's church, then under construction (on the left just behind the horse and cart).

102 A fascinating shop interior of premises at 20 High Street owned by Herbert Saunders, grocer and ship's biscuit manufacturer, *c*.1918. Because they were near the quay, such stores had valuable victualling contracts.

103 Some goods were brought to the door. The delivery carts, milk churns and quart and gill dipper measures of dairies were a familiar sight. One of these was Chalkley's Dairy (pictured in 1906), now John Bates' Tyre Depot in Commercial Road. Malmesbury and Parsons Dairy, further up Commercial Road, was then known as Parkstone Dairy.

FRIED FISH BAR,

13, High Street, Poole

Mrs. WEST

Thanks the Residents of Poole and its vicinity for the generous support they have given her during the past eight years, and she hopes to merit a continuance of the same. She will personally superintend all fish and materials used in cooking same, and guarantees everything used shall continue to be of the very best quality; she will also study to satisfy all her Customers, and all Children sent by their Parents will be carefully served. She is also adding a daily supply of Wet Fish, direct from Grimsby, to be sold cheaply as possible during the day.

March
April
July
Aug.
Oct.

HOT FRIED FISH AND

CHIP POTATOES

from **6.30** to **10.30** every night.

SHOPS SUPPLIED.

Inspection invited at all times.

104 Forget Harry Ramsden's! Poole has a long tradition of good fish and chips. As Mrs. West promises, 'All children sent by parents will be carefully served'.

105 Millers of Poole are renowned for their sausages and pork pies, but an earlier sausage manufacturer was Godwin's, with premises in New Quay Road and a shop in the High Street.

106 High Street at the Longfleet end in the 1880s. Shops mix with houses, including the store of Burden's, grocer's, on the right, which had been established in the 1850s. The jeweller's on the left was Edward John Counsell's, and closed in 1890. This area now lies beneath Falkland Square, Tescos, Boots and Littlewoods.

107 Town centre shopping was transformed with the opening of Arndale (now Dolphin) Centre in 1969. The scheme was chosen after competition by a majority of only one vote in council; the members voted then 'in the interests of the town' and not on party lines. 'Arndale' was a composite name from the founders, Mr. Argenbach and Bradford's Sam Chippendale.

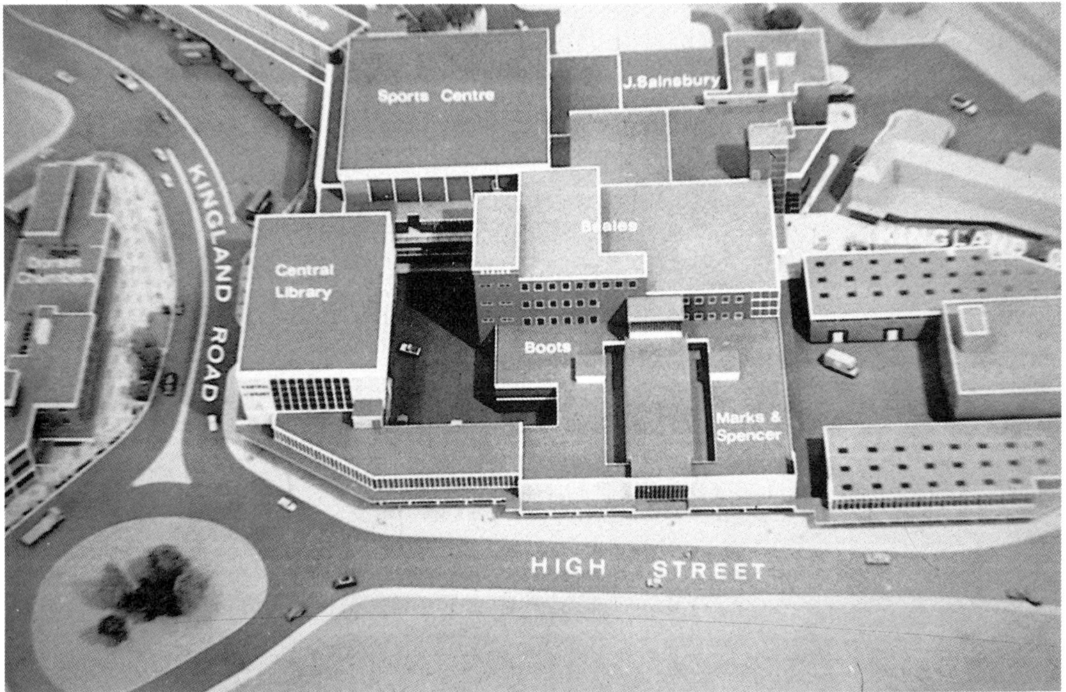

Worship

108 Canford church includes the oldest buildings in the borough (11th century) and was the progenitor of the present 19 parishes (some combined). As a royal peculiar it could conduct legal business, including proving wills. Nowadays it only retains the privilege (with St James') that choristers wear scarlet cassocks.

109 In 1550 old service books were banned from the Church of England. The vellum pages, useless for church purposes, were used to cover paper documents. This Poole antiphonal dated *c.*1350 relating to the feast of SS Philip and James was the cover to 1598 overseers' accounts.

110 The Temperance Hall, Hill Street, built in the late 1860s, was not a church, but housed a fervent movement. The evil of drink fired leading Liberal councillors George Curtis, estate agent and Wesleyan preacher, and John J. Norton, timber merchant, to seek (but not obtain) a ban on Sunday sales against Conservative brewery interests in the 1880s.

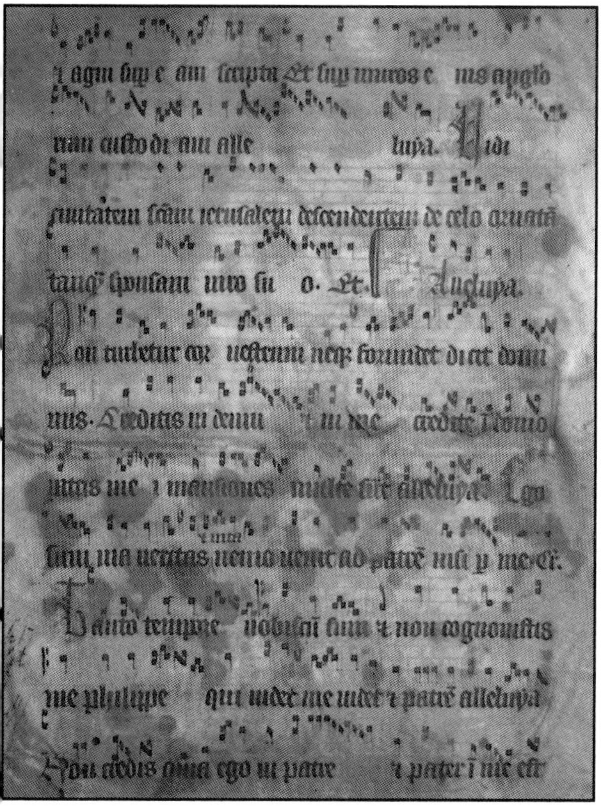

111 The former church of St Michael's, Hamworthy was built in 1826 (demolished 1964) on the site of a medieval church pulled down in the Civil War. The stone was used to provide Poole's Parliamentarians with a landward defence against royalist attack. Nearby Hamworthy rectory is the oldest brick-built house in Dorset. The Duke of Wellington lodged in it.

112 Parkstone Congregational Church (1893) designed by Mr. Donkin of Bournemouth cost £3,050; the spire has now been demolished for safety. An earlier church (1839) paid for by Mrs. Bunn (whose maiden name was Buckland) later served as Parkstone British School and then as the church hall for St Peter's Church.

113 This photograph can be exactly dated to 29 May 1907. It was taken at the laying of the foundation-stone of Loch Road Baptist Church, carried out by J. J. Allen J.P. Messrs. Jones and Seward of Bournemouth were the builders of the tabernacle at a cost of £3,500.

114 The interior of St Peter's church in 1908. The description 'Poole's Cathedral' is often applied to this, the largest church in Poole. In 1912 Sir Robert Baden Powell, who founded the Scout Movement on nearby Brownsea Island, was married to Olave Soames (whose family lived at Grey Rigg, Parkstone) in the church.

115 This 1855 Brannon engraving shows St Mary's, Brownsea Island, a year after its completion. Panelling in the church came from Richard III's Council Chamber in Bishopsgate. No clergyman has ever held the living and the church has to be served by the rector of St Peter's who crosses by boat.

116 An uncompleted church (it lacks a campanile) is St Aldhelm's. It was designed in late 'Decorated' style by G. F. Bodley and celebrated its centenary in 1994.

117 St John's church, Broadstone cost £2,500 and was dedicated in 1888. Broadstone had been opened up by the railway, and was the nearest station to Canford and to much of Poole. Lord Wimborne realised its potential and sold building plots. He paid for the nave and heating of the church.

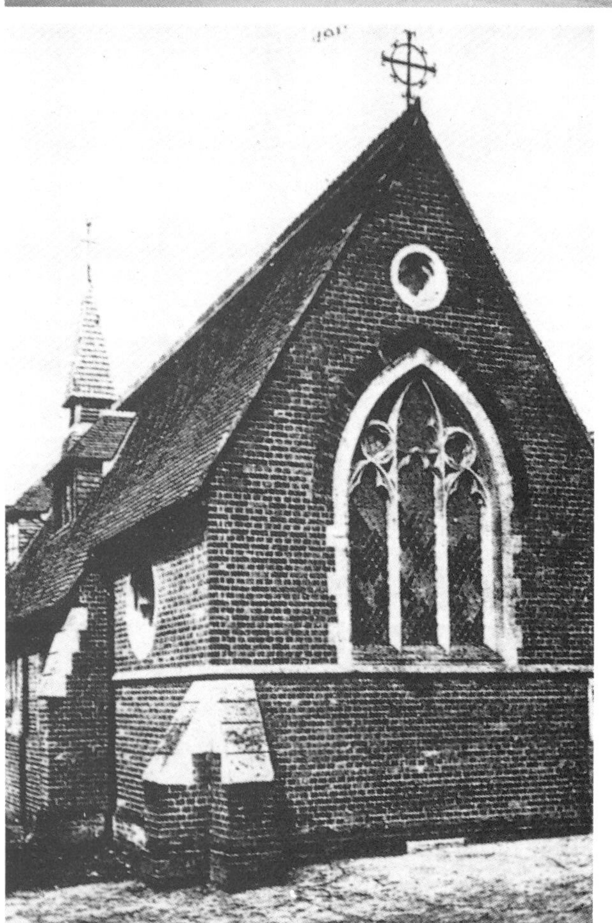

118 The original St Aldhelm's School (shown) was a mission to pottery workers created by Rev. Alexander Morden-Bennett, vicar of St Peter's Bournemouth, who crossed civil and diocesan boundaries to carry out this work. The schoolroom doubled as a church on Sundays. It has now been demolished.

119 The interior of the Chapel of Holy Angels, Lilliput, pictured in 1908. Described by Pevsner as a 'horrid chapel in buff brick', the rood screen, choir stalls and organ case were designed by Bodley. The chapel commemorates the Butts family, a member of which had been a patron of Turner and built an art gallery in Antony's Avenue.

120 St Osmund's church, in Byzantine style, was the last designed by E. S. Prior, built between 1913 and 1916 as an addition to an earlier chancel (constructed in 1904) and completed in 1927. The interior contains inscriptions by Eric Gill and glass by MacDonald Gill, his brother.

121 Roman Catholics were served by emigre priests at a mission in Wimborne Road until, in 1837, Edward Doughty (later Baron Tichborne) of Upton House built St Mary and St Philomena's church in West Quay Road, served by his personal chaplain, as a thanksgiving for the recovery of his daughter from an illness. The church, demolished in 1973 for the RNLI headquarters, was visible from Upton House two miles away.

122 The completed St Mary's, Longfleet, is shown in this photograph of a contemporary funeral. St Mary's had been associated with the Liberal cause and 'low' church in the 1800s, and St Peter's, Parkstone, with the Conservatives and Tractarians or 'high' church.

123 The developing area of Oakdale merited a new church (pictured) in 1932. The foundation-stone laying ceremony of St George's took place on 30 September 1932. Herbert Kendall, Diocesan Surveyor, stands to the right of the scaffolding. This building became the church hall when a new church, dedicated in 1960, was built alongside it.

124 Because of offensive smells from uncovered coffins under the floor, St James' church was rebuilt in 1817-21. The cost was a source of controversy as there were fears that the church rate would be increased to pay for it. Even the contractor had to explain he had made a loss, to add to his losses in Newfoundland.

TO THE

INHABITANTS OF POOLE.

THE circumstances respecting my situation and property when I first came to Poole, and when I contracted to build your new Church, the loss which I and my Creditors have sustained in the Erection of that Building, (without meaning to reflect upon any one,) being altogether unknown to many of you and being I fear misunderstood by some; you will not I hope deem it intrusive in me to lay before you the real state of the case, for although I have been unfortunate, yet I wish to convince you that I never had an intention to injure any one.

The Cash which I brought with me to Poole and which I received afterwards before I began to build the Church, amounted to £1250 besides Household Furniture of the value of £80, and I have lost the whole of this sum (except about one hundred and fifty pounds which I lost by a fire at St. Johns) in building the Church, besides a heavy loss which my Creditors sustained; I owed no money whatever when I came to Poole, for I first started in business here; and I never paid any debts on account of my Father as it has been insinuated.

I am ready to verify these facts, and to prove the accuracy of the following statement, as far as concerns myself, and I presume the statement is correct as to the monies received by my Assignees or due to them.

THOS. BENHAM.

Dr. *T. BENHAM for Cash Paid and Received on Account of* POOLE CHURCH AND TOWER, *Cr.*

	£	s.	d.		£	s.	d.
Paid for Materials	5,990	19	4	Received of the Committee and Churchwardens...	9,711	0	0
—— Wages	3,620	3	6½	Balance of Cash paid more than received	846	7	8½
—— Sundry Accounts	946	4	10				
	£ 10,557	7	8½		£ 10,557	7	8½

Abstract of Profit and Loss by the Contract.

	£	s.	d.		£	s.	d.
To Payments as above	10,557	7	8½	By Receipts as above....	9,711	0	0
Sundry Bills now due to my Creditors....	2,929	5	2½	Cash my Assignees received from the Committee and Churchwardens........	1,041	14	3
				Ditto from Sale of Old Materials, &c..........	372	0	0
				Balance lost..........	2,361	18	8
	£ 13,486	12	11		£ 13,486	12	11

125 The interior of St James' church, looking towards the gallery, displays columns constructed from Newfoundland pine. In 1844 the church's brass chandeliers were sold and shipped to St Peter's church, Twillingate, Newfoundland, where they remain. St Peter's is willing to return them—in exchange for the pine columns!

Parish of St. James,

POOLE.

Notice is hereby Given, that a MEETING of the Inhabitants will be holden at the Vestry, on FRIDAY the Fifteenth of June, instant, at 10 o'clock in the Forenoon, at the toll of the Bell, to determine on the mode of appointing an ORGANIST, MR. JOSEPH GOSS having signified his intention of resigning at Midsummer next.

WILLIAM HILL, } *Church-*
THOMAS G. HANCOCK, } *wardens.*

June 9, 1838.

By the above judicious Notice of the Churchwardens, posted yesterday on the Church Doors, the Inhabitants must see the propriety of giving to each Candidate for the situation, Fair Play, by testing their merit before competent Judges, and every honest straightforward Rate-payer should attend the Vestry, and carry out such well meant intentions so as to secure to the Parish, the most competent and efficient Organist.

A RATE-PAYER.

J. SYDENHAM, PRINTER, POOLE.

126 Democracy ruled at the 1838 selection of a replacement organist! The organ had been a gift from Benjamin Lester, Newfoundland merchant, in 1799. The parish clerk of St James' from 1729-68 was William Knapp, composer of the hymn tune 'Wareham'.

127 Not all religion is orthodox. George Tucker was a well-known itinerant preacher. The side of his van proclaims, 'Be sure your sins will find you out. The wicked shall be turned into Hell. Come unto me and I will give you rest. When I see the blood I will pass over you. I will trust and not be afraid'.

Road, Rail and Air

128 The road routes to and from Poole were limited, as seen on this extract from Bowen's map of 1763. The route via Wimborne was used for London and via Longham for all points to the east. Bournemouth did not then exist and the Great Heath and Bourne Stream were skirted.

129 In 1675 John Ogilby, His Majesty's Cosmographer, produced very practical ribbon maps for travellers based on surveys. This one shows, from bottom right to top left, the road from Oxford to Poole via Salisbury, a distance of 87 miles and three furlongs. Junctions are shown and hills represent upwards or downwards slopes pictorially. The main road from Poole to Christchurch was via Canford Bridge.

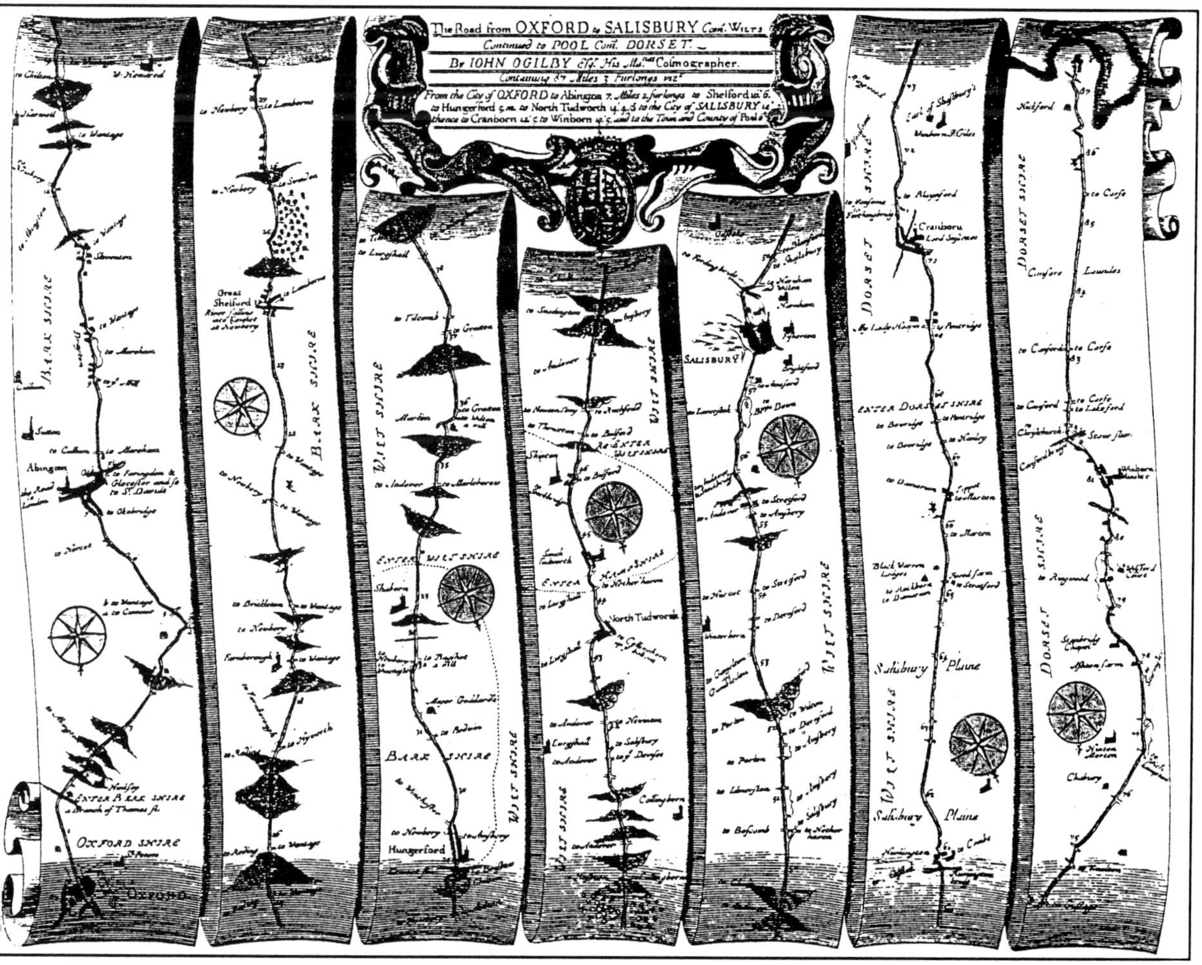

130 The Turnpike Trusts established in the mid-1700s were promoted to increase trade and travel. Such routes are usually still major roads. This toll house stood at the entrance to the town at the junction of the Longfleet and Wimborne Roads in front of the *George Hotel* until 1926. Tolls had been abolished in 1882. The poster on the fence is part of the recruitment campaign for Kitchener's Army and announces 'The Army would suit You'. After the First World War the tollhouse also served as the depot for the sale of newspapers on Sundays, as shops did not then open on the Sabbath.

131 This road layout pictured from the air looks planned, but uninhabited by cars. The centre of this pre-war picture is the *New Inn* at Oakdale, where a variety of traffic schemes have been tried over the years to improve flows and reduce accidents, ranging from the roundabout seen here, to complex traffic lights and one-way streets. The area then supported a number of smallholdings and nurseries, which have since been built upon.

132 Many of today's main roads were unmade or gravel surfaced. This is almost unbelievably the now busy junction of Sea View Road and Ringwood Road (then referred to as Poole Road) pictured in a postcard at the turn of the century. Until the 1960s many roads were made up with gravel over a heather base to aid drainage.

133 Lord Wimborne pictured at the wheel of his motor car in 1902 at Canford. Lady Wimborne was driven separately by her chauffeur in the vehicle behind. Perhaps she did not trust his driving?

134 Charles Trent of Newtown made a business of disposing of old cars and boasted 'the largest dump' in the British Isles. Nearby was the Limmer and Trinidad Asphalt works, which provided the material for surfacing roads. Trinidad Estate is named from this —there is no West Indian connection.

135 Road-making in the Ashley Road in 1907. This Edison Road Roller was driven by S. R. Dodge and is pictured outside the Castle Stores of Alfred Hazzard, beer retailer.

136 Poole pioneered a tram service to County Gates in 1901 using overhead power. Bournemouth vigorously opposed trams that year, but later adopted a conduit system, bought the Poole company and inaugurated a service to Bournemouth Square on 3 July 1905. The mayor of Bournemouth, Ald. Beale, is seen travelling in the luxurious Tram No.1, fitted with curtains and wicker armchairs. The first week's takings were just under £140.

137 The Poole-bound tram leaving Christchurch in 1905, the year a through service was started.

138 In 1847 railways reached Hamworthy (the first Poole station) from Wimborne. In 1849 the London and South Western Railway introduced a steamship service taking 5½ hours to the Channel Islands. A main cabin cost 21s. and one cwt. of luggage could be taken free!

139 For the railway to cross the river Stour a bridge and embankment had to be constructed. This marvel of the iron road was sketched in 1847 for the *Illustrated London News*. The line, known as Castleman's Corkscrew, was initially the only railway route to London for both Poole and Bournemouth.

140 The picture on the left shows the railway viaducts at Bourne Valley under construction in 1884. 520,000 cubic yards of soil were removed and tipped to form embankments. A variety of steam equipment used in railway construction reduced the need for railway 'navvies'. Mowlem's were the contractors, and William Jacomb the Chief Engineer. A horse and cart are reputed to have toppled into the 'fill' and were lost.

141 The *Somerset and Dorset* (or 'Slow and Dirty' as it was known) is here seen (below left) running from Holes Bay junction en route to Bath. It was a popular route for holiday-makers and excursions, until it suffered the fate of many others under the Beeching axe.

142 Poole quay was reached by a branch line running down West Quay Road from Poole station. It reached a peak of activity in the preparations for D-Day. This photograph (below) is one of the last to show the line being worked, in 1954.

143 From pre-war Imperial Airways days until BOAC withdrew to Hythe in 1948, Poole was a flying-boat base. From the Wareham Channel flights took off for the first stage of journeys to Durban, Karachi and Auckland. This photograph shows an Imperial Airways plane being worked at Hamworthy.

School days

144 One of the first 'paid' (½d. per week) schools in Parkstone was set up in 1865 by Martin Luther Preston at 'Heather-lands' in Dunford Road. This photograph is believed to be of Martin Luther Preston with a violin which he made from a South African war bully beef tin.

145 When this class photograph was taken in 1902 Branksome Heath School, built in 1874 and enlarged in 1890, was known as Kinson Heath Church of England School and occupied premises in Croft Road.

146 The Parade in Parkstone Road in 1908, showing Church House on the left, a school financed by William Ernest Brennand, a wealthy resident of Parkstone, which opened in 1904. The Rev. Stanley Moss of St Peter's was Headmaster, with one assistant, Miss Beale. Mr. Brennand died in 1912 leaving the school mortgaged. It somehow survived until Dorset County took over in 1932.

147 Church House was later known as Parkstone Grammar School for Girls, now in Soper's Lane, and Ashley Cross Girls' School. The building is currently being preserved in a redevelopment, but only the door is original. The rest had to be rebuilt in 1953 as it had become unsafe.

148 Poole Secondary School was established in Mount Street in 1904. In 1907 it occupied these new buildings in Kingland Road (criticised as 'squat') on a site given by Lord Wimborne. As Poole Grammar School from 1927, and restricted to boys in 1939, the premises became Seldown Boys' School from 1966 until that school transferred to Ashdown School.

149 The National (i.e. Church of England) School (St James') was founded at Perry Gardens in Lagland Street (opposite Globe Lane) in 1835 and closed in 1939. It charged 2d. a week. In January 1917, a very severe winter, the wooden lavatory seats dis-appeared and were thought to have been used as firewood by needy persons in the town. National School 'fleas' often fought the 'bugs' from the nearby British (i.e. Nonconformist) School.

150 An 1835 watercolour of Canford Manor which was then a private house before it became Canford School in 1923. The school recently obtained £7.7m for the last of the Assyrian bas-reliefs excavated by Sir Henry Layard and presented to his father-in-law for display in the house. Lord Wimborne had sold others to New York's Metropolitan Museum in 1919.

151 Henry Harbin pupils of H. P. Smith examine artefacts from school 'digs'. With the help of pupils a Roman pottery at Hamworthy was examined as well as the line of the Roman road. H. P. Smith prepared a number of teaching aids to train these young archaeologists.

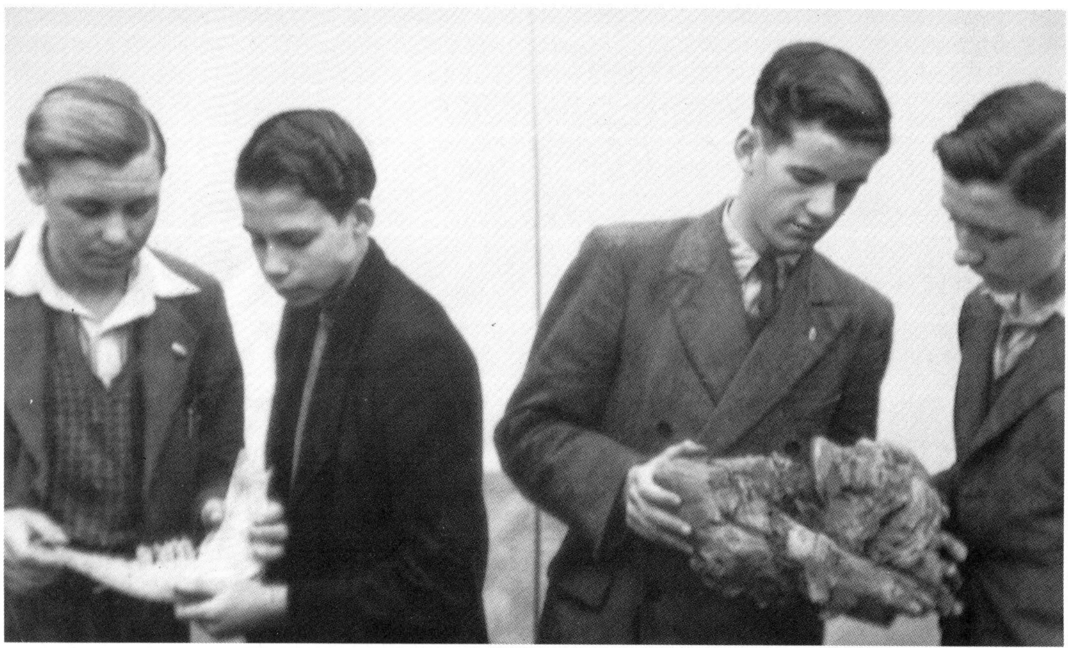

Working in the Borough

This Indenture, made the Fourteenth Day of July in the Thirty first Year of the Reign of our Sovereign Lord George the second by the Grace of God, of Great Britain, France, and Ireland, King Defender of the Faith, and so forth, and in the Year of our Lord 1757 Witnesseth, That George Bidoul and James Chinnock Church-wardens of the Parish of Sherborne in the County of Dorset and George Sarsery and John Glover Overseers of the Poor of the said Parish by and with the Consent of his Majesty's Justices of the Peace for the said County of Dorset whose Names are hereunto subscrib'd, have put and plac'd, and by these Presents do put and place John Healy aged Thirteen years or thereabouts, a poor Child of the said Parish Apprentice to Messrs Brooks & Lemon of Poole in the County of Dorset Merchants with them to dwell and serve from the Day of the Date of these Presents, until the said Apprentice shall accomplish his full Age of Twenty one Years according to the Statute in that Case made and provided: During all which Term, the said Apprentice his said Master faithfully shall serve in all lawful Businesses according to his Power, Wit and Ability; and honestly, orderly and obediently in all Things demean and behave him-self towards his said Masters and all theirs during the said Term. And the said Messrs Brooks & Lemon for them-self, their Executors and Administrators, doth Covenant and Grant to and with the said Church-wardens and Overseers, and every of them, their, and every of their Executors and Administrators, and their and every of their Successors, for the Time being, by these Presents, That the said John Healy the said Apprentice in the Art or Mystery of Seafaring, Fishing and curing Fish will teach or cause to be taught and instructed And shall and will, during all the Term aforesaid, find, provide, and allow unto the said Apprentice meet, competent, and sufficient Meat, Drink, Apparel, Lodging, Washing, and all other Things necessary and fit for an Apprentice: And also shall and will so provide for the said Apprentice, that he be not any way a Charge to the said Parish or Parishioners of the same; but of and from all Charge shall and will save the said Parish and Parishioners thereof harmless and indemnify'd during the said Term: and at the End of the said Term shall and will make and provide and deliver unto the said Apprentice a good and new Suit of Apparel of all Sorts In Witness whereof, the Parties abovesaid to these present Indentures interchangeably have set their Hands and Seals the Day and Year first above-written.

We whose Names are here under-written, Justices of the Peace for the County of Dorset aforesaid (whereof one is of the Quorum) Do consent to the putting forth the abovesaid John Healy Apprentice, according to the Intent and Meaning of the above Indenture.

Sealed and delivered in the Presence of

the Mark of

Lemon & Brooks

152 To avoid charges on the parish, the poor or orphans were apprenticed to the Newfoundland trade. In 1757 James Chinnock, aged 13, was apprenticed until he was 21 to Brookes and Lemon, merchants, to learn the 'mystery of seafaring, fishing and curing fish'.

153 A workman would not see many of these £10 notes. Fryer's bank, founded in 1790, had links with Isaac Gulliver, as his daughter married into the family with a reputed £100,000 dowry derived from his smuggling activities; a useful source of 'laundered' capital for the bank! The bank merged with National Provincial in 1840 and is now part of NatWest.

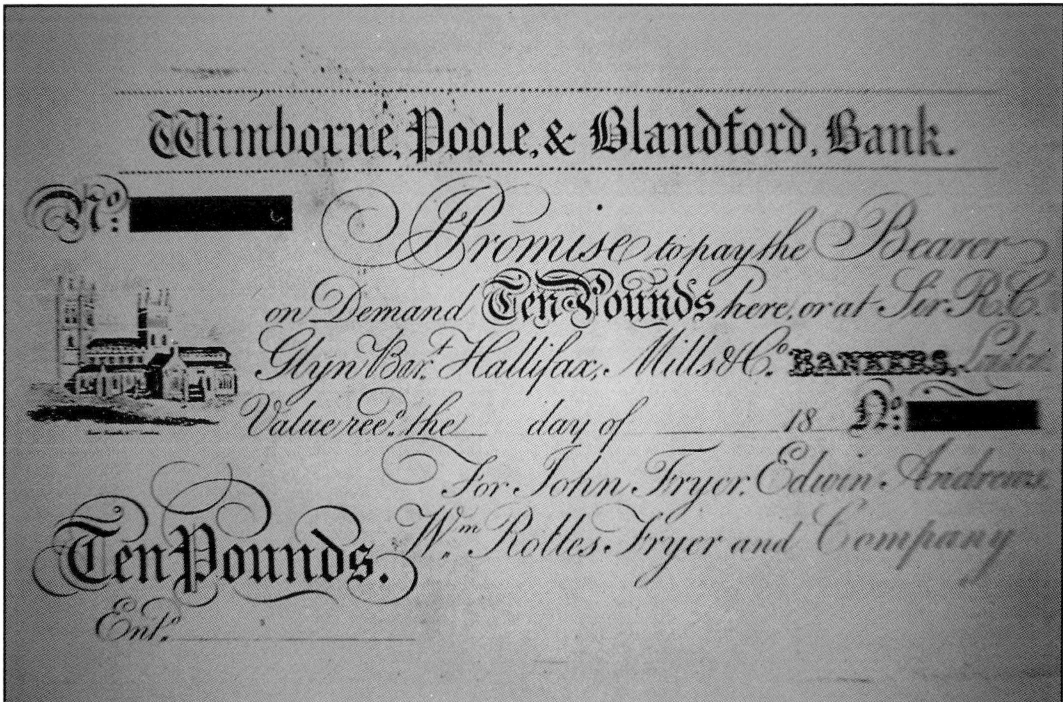

Wimborne, Poole, & Blandford, Bank.

No.

Promise to pay the Bearer on Demand Ten Pounds here, or at Sir R. C. Glyn Bart. Hallifax, Mills & Co. BANKERS, London

Value recd. the day of 18 No.

For John Fryer, Edwin Andrews, Wm. Rolles Fryer and Company

Ten Pounds.

Entd.

E VALLEY POTTERY.

154 This aerial view, left, shows the old lifeboat station and the area traditionally used by fishermen for drying nets. On an unreclaimed Baiter (site of the plague burials, the town gallows and the windmill) the isolation hospital, last used in 1936, is visible but not the unmarked ruin of the Powder House which still exists on the shoreline.

155 The Bourne Valley Pottery (later known as Sharp Jones), below left, at Pottery Junction made glazed earthenware drainage pipes. This photograph dates from *c*.1936. Kinson Pottery also made such pipes and obtained a large order from Argentina in 1910.

156 The railway to Poole via Wimborne (below) carried bulk goods as well as passengers. Workers are photographed unloading coal from LSWR wagons at Oakley, which still retains rural surroundings, if not haystacks. A High Court decision in the 1960s permitted housing development on 100 acres of the former Oakley flying field.

157 In the late 1920s a number of roads in the area were made up as projects to relieve unemployment, half the cost being met by the Government. The famous 'switchback' of Alder Road (pictured left) was one of these schemes. Workers taking a break include Mr Bendall (marked).

158 Staff of Poole Gasworks pictured below left, *c*.1860. The man in the top hat is Martin Kemp Welch (1804-87), who was Secretary to the company and a solicitor. To his left is the accountant Joseph Barter. John Budden, the manager and superintendent, is on the right wearing a bowler hat.

159 These stokers at the Bourne Valley Gasworks (below) were pictured 30 years later in 1890. The headgear had changed and fashion dictated the demise of the waistcoat.

160 Even though steam equipment was available, the days of the horse and tipping cart had not passed, as this 1884 photograph shows. The size of the task of building the Bourne Valley viaducts can be gauged from the amount of soil tipped for the embankment.

161 The gasholder features in this 1906 picture of W. Scott's cart crossing the Bournemouth railway loop in the vicinity of Guest Avenue.

162 This engine used to work the line to Jennings' South Western Pottery, seen in the background, and carries the name *George Jennings*. A branch line led to Parkstone-by-Sea station, which advertised the area as 'England's Mentone'.

163 Many farms and nursery gardens existed around Poole (including a lavender farm at Broadstone). Viney's farm at Blake Dene at the turn of the century was captured in this water-colour painting by the artist, Arnold Knight. Knight, who was disabled, lived nearby. The Viney family now have a horticultural business at Parkstone.

164 Many houses supported domestic staff, either living in, or as 'dailies'. Upton House, dating from the 1790s, supported the 11 staff seen here in 1910 to carry out domestic duties and look after the grounds. The live-in staff occupied rooms in the attic with their own staircase to aid their movements to fill coal scuttles or answer bells.

165 At Viney's farm at Blake Dene strawberry time was a busy occasion, packing the produce for market in traditional punnets.

166 Viney's milk float on its rounds. The milkman always welcomed young helpers—in this case his son, Stan Viney. In later years the firm also had a coal business, distributing in the area.

Harbour and Shipping

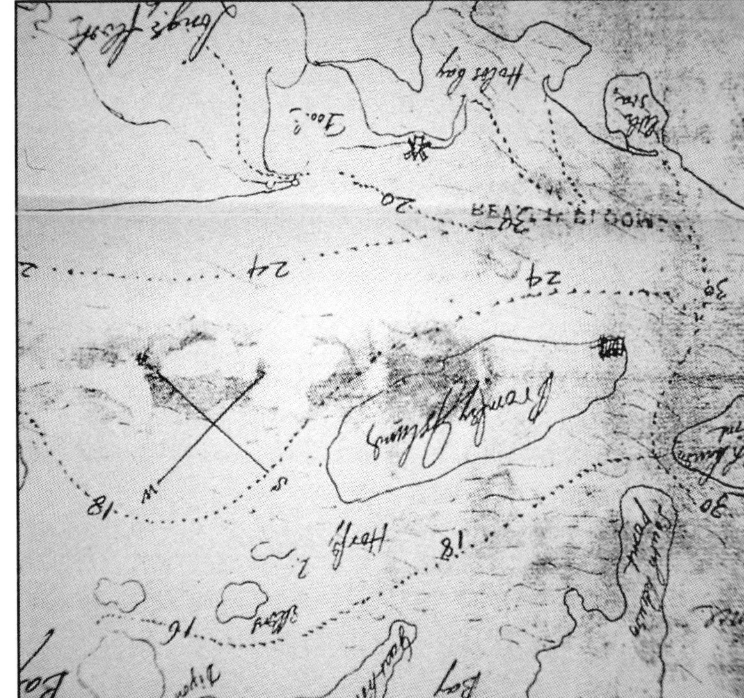

167 A chart prepared in 1662 is the earliest to show detail of Poole harbour. Apart from the windmill at Baiter it shows Holes Bay in its correct position (it was transposed with Longfleet Bay in later maps) and soundings of depths.

168 In 1745 Sir Peter Thompson had a survey drawn which confirmed the position of Holes Bay and refers to Longfleet Bay as 'the water within Poole'. By the time of the Sheringham survey in 1849 (illustrated) the error in the location of Holes Bay had been established and it has remained thus ever since.

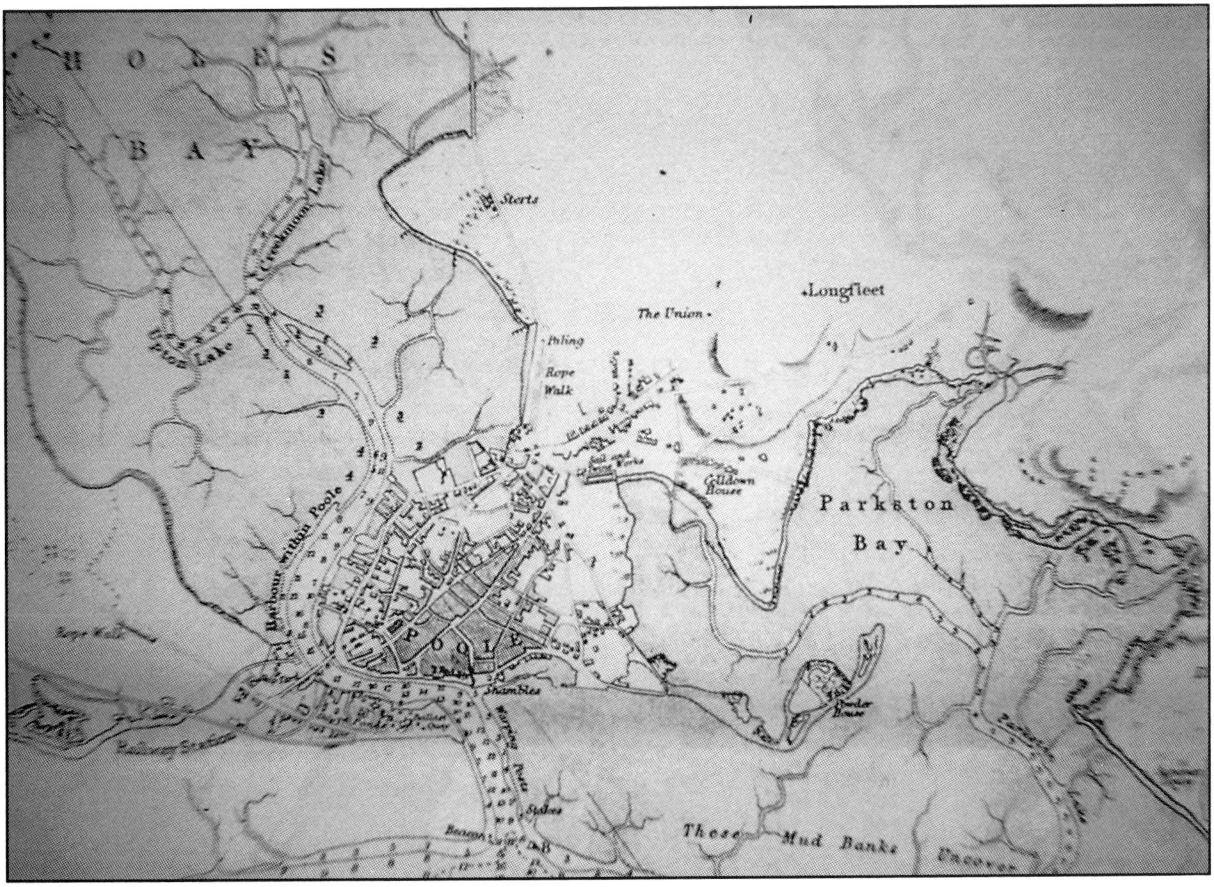

169 By 1860 the Newfoundland trade had ceased and the quay appears very inactive in this print. Even the famous native oyster fishery of Poole had collapsed, through overfishing. Defoe had described Poole's as 'the best and biggest oysters' which were pickled and sent in barrels all over the world. Henry Hastings, Squire of Woodlands, ate them twice a day all year round. There was not a woman around under the age of 40, 'but it was her own fault if he was not intimately acquanted with her!'.

170 The Brig *David* (138 tons), portrayed in 1864, was built in Poole in 1850 by Miller and Meadus for Thomas and David Slade. Under captain Peter Moore she undertook voyages to Labrador and returned via the Mediterranean. She collided with a steamship in thick fog off the Scillies in 1869.

171 This 1833 engraving depicts a busy quay. The oyster fishery was, however, in serious decline despite measures by the council to limit catches. Much of the quay area is built on banks of discarded shells several feet thick. Oysters were not regarded as a luxury food, but one for poor people. In the 20th century the industry was revived using cultivated oysters, most of which are exported.

172 The Ham Side traditionally provided the shipyards and careening facilities, and was where ballast was loaded or discharged. This engraving dates from *c.*1840. Until Poole Harbour Commissioners were set up in 1895, the council, as Trustees of the Quays, ran the harbour.

173 By 1890 a mixture of sail and steam could be seen on Poole quay. Most of the vessels were bound only on continental or coastal voyages and clay was the major export. The draught for vessels was restricted and only improved after the creation of Poole Training Bank, approved after the Wolfe Barry report in 1923, which aroused great controversy.

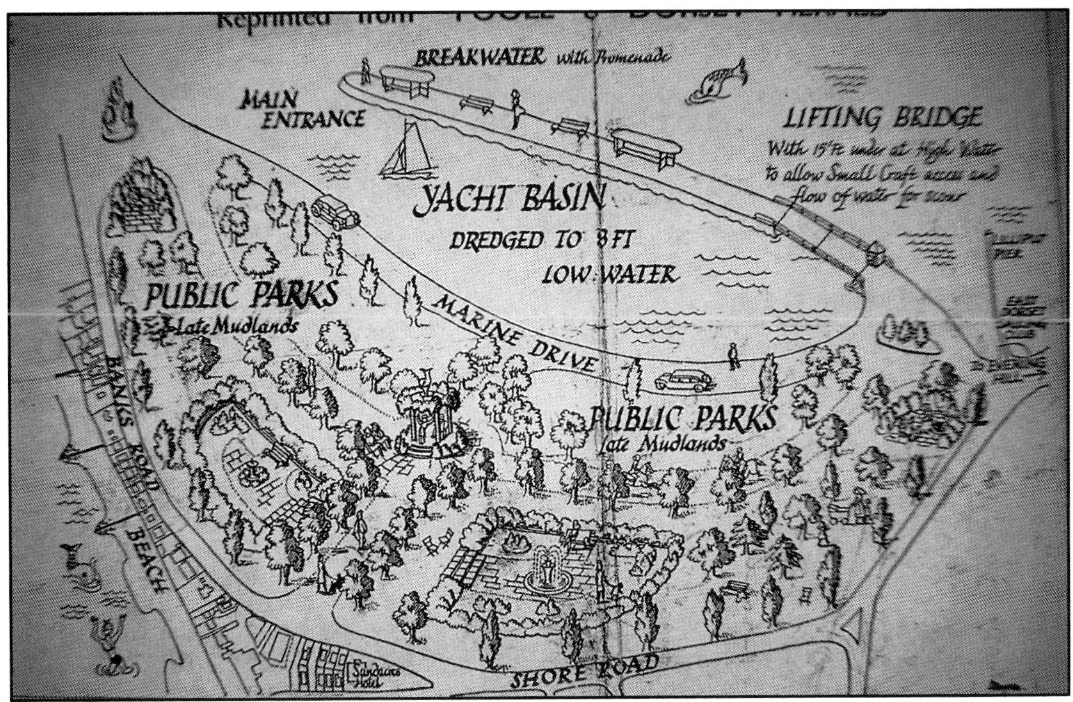

174 Equally controversial was this 1946 plan to fill in part of the harbour for a yacht basin. In the 1950s a proposal to fill in this area for additional car parking was even more vociferously turned down.

175 The channels of the harbour have needed regular dredging for commercial traffic. In 1929 the aptly named steam dredger *Shifter* performed this task. After the War three former landing craft, renamed *Hop*, *Skip* and *Jump*, were scuttled near this point to form a breakwater before reclamation took place.

176 Fine sailing vessels could still be seen in Poole after the turn of the century. In this picture Sydenham's timber yard can be seen above the old Poole Bridge.

177 Several firms offered voyages to Torquay, Portsmouth and the Isle of Wight. The paddler *Brodrick Castle* (Capt. Tilsed), in service with the Bournemouth and South Coast Steam Packet Co. from 1887 to 1909, was described as the 'fastest and most powerful vessel on the South Coast', but in fact was not licensed, as others were, to cross the Channel.

178 Trips on the *Skylark* were always popular with visitors (as tourists were then politely called). Jake Bolson's cry of 'Any more for the *Skylark*' is legendary. Bolson's family firm built these boats, and are now ship repairers. Their yard, which adjoins the birthplace of Hamworthy Engineering, has now passed into the hands of Poole Harbour Commissioners.

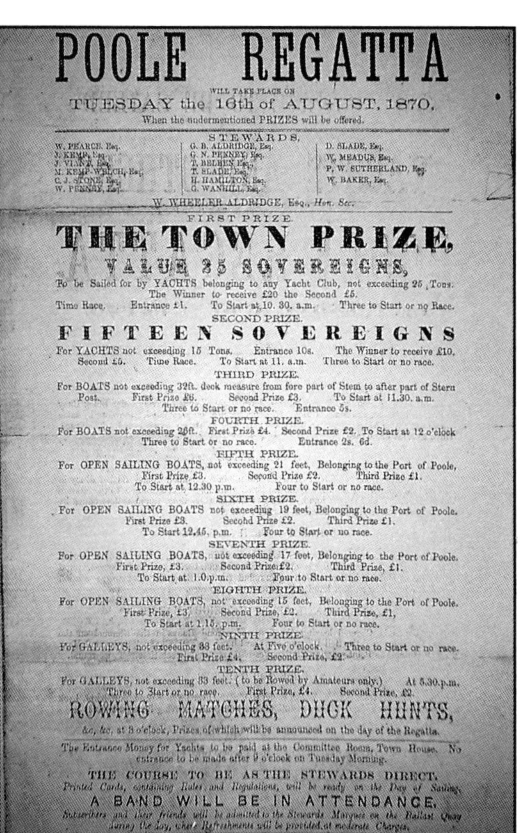

POOLE REGATTA

WILL TAKE PLACE ON

TUESDAY the 16th of AUGUST, 1870,

When the undermentioned PRIZES will be offered.

STEWARDS.

W. PEARCE, Esq.	G. B. ALDRIDGE, Esq.	D. SLADE, Esq.
J. KEMP, Esq.	G. N. PENNEY, Esq.	W. MEADUS, Esq.
J. VIANE, Esq.	T. BELBEN, Esq.	P. W. SUTHERLAND, Esq.
M. KEMP-WELCH, Esq.	T. SLADE, Esq.	W. BAKER, Esq.
C. J. STONE, Esq.	H. HAMILTON, Esq.	
W. PENNEY, Esq.	G. WANHILL, Esq.	

W. WHEELER ALDRIDGE, Esq., *Hon. Sec.*

FIRST PRIZE.

THE TOWN PRIZE,

VALUE 25 SOVEREIGNS,

To be Sailed for by YACHTS belonging to any Yacht Club, not exceeding 25 Tons.
The Winner to receive £20 the Second £5.
Time Race. Entrance £1. To Start at 10. 30. a.m. Three to Start or no Race.

SECOND PRIZE.

FIFTEEN SOVEREIGNS

For YACHTS not exceeding 15 Tons. Entrance 10s. The Winner to receive £10.
Second £5. Time Race. To Start at 11. a.m. Three to Start or no race.

THIRD PRIZE.

For BOATS not exceeding 32ft. deck measure from fore part of Stem to after part of Stern Post. First Prize £6. Second Prize £3. To Start at 11.30. a.m.
Three to Start or no race. Entrance 5s.

FOURTH PRIZE.

For BOATS not exceeding 26ft. First Prize £4. Second Prize £2. To Start at 12 o'clock
Three to Start or no race. Entrance 2s. 6d.

FIFTH PRIZE.

For OPEN SAILING BOATS, not exceeding 21 feet, Belonging to the Port of Poole,
First Prize £3. Second Prize £2. Third Prize £1.
To Start at 12.30 p.m. Four to Start or no race.

SIXTH PRIZE.

For OPEN SAILING BOATS not exceeding 19 feet, Belonging to the Port of Poole.
First Prize £3. Second Prize £2. Third Prize £1.
To Start 12.45. p.m. Four to Start or no race.

SEVENTH PRIZE.

For OPEN SAILING BOATS, not exceeding 17 feet, Belonging to the Port of Poole.
First Prize, £3. Second Prize £2. Third Prize, £1.
To Start at 1.0.p.m. Four to Start or no race.

EIGHTH PRIZE.

For OPEN SAILING BOATS, not exceeding 15 feet, Belonging to the Port of Poole.
First Prize, £3. Second Prize, £2. Third Prize, £1,
To Start at 1.15. p.m. Four to Start or no race.

NINTH PRIZE.

For GALLEYS, not exceeding 33 feet. At Five o'clock. Three to Start or no race.
First Prize £4. Second Prize, £2.

TENTH PRIZE.

For GALLEYS, not exceeding 33 feet. (to be Rowed by Amateurs only.) At 5.30.p.m.
Three to Start or no race. First Prize, £4. Second Prize, £2.

ROWING MATCHES, DUCK HUNTS,

&c, &c, at 3 o'clock, Prizes of which will be announced on the day of the Regatta.

The Entrance Money for Yachts to be paid at the Committee Room, Town House. No entrance to be made after 9 o'clock on Tuesday Morning.

THE COURSE TO BE AS THE STEWARDS DIRECT.

Printed Cards, containing Rules and Regulations, will be ready on the Day of Sailing.

A BAND WILL BE IN ATTENDANCE.

Subscribers and their friends will be admitted to the Stewards Marquee on the Ballast Quay during the day, where Refreshments will be provided at moderate Charges.

WOODFORD, PRINTER, POOLE.

179 Private yachting was an important part of the harbour scene. As early as 1855 regattas were held, with suitable entertainment, bands etc., and prizes for the winners. Poole Week is the modern equivalent, but nothing could equal the days of the large yachts, including the *'J'* class, which raced in Poole Bay in the early years of the century.

180 Parkstone Sailing Club and pier as they were, *c.*1907. The main club house remained in use as a boat-shed for Parkstone Yacht Club, as it is now called, until recent years. The club is now building a yacht haven.

181 The *Florinda* (far left), built in 1874 and one of the 'big five' of her day, moored at Poole quay, was the clubhouse of the Royal Motor Yacht Club before it took premises by the Old Coastguard Cottages at Sandbanks in 1936. It was Regatta Day and the committee boat was disembarking passengers.

182 One of the major trophies of motor boating, the Harmsworth Trophy, presented by Lord Northcliffe in 1903, is housed at the RMYC. It was the first trophy for a race for power boats, which then achieved speeds of 20 mph!

183 Motor boat racing off Poole quay in the 1930s. The old pottery kiln and the coal transporter for the gasworks can be seen in the background.

184 In 1947 Malcolm Campbell used Poole harbour for speed trials of his *Bluebird K4*. In 1934 Hubert Scott-Paine broke the world salt-water speed record in Poole when he obtained 110mph from *Miss Great Britain III*.

185 In 1948, when this picture was taken, fishermen were still using in-shore boats, drying and mending their nets on the shore and hawking their fish around the local pubs.

186 Going, going ... . It took 80lbs of explosive to fell the 325ft. octagonal chimneys of Poole Generating Station. Ten thousand people watched as the two chimneys toppled.

187 Gone ... . Fourteen thousand tons of steel and locally made bricks crashed to the ground. All that remains on the site, now that the dust has settled, is a 150,000-ton slab of concrete.

188 The heyday of Poole in many people's estimation was the late 1930s. Here fine beach facilities at Branksome Chine lie within reach of luxurious private houses in large grounds and an even more luxurious hotel at Branksome Tower.

BOROUGH of
POOLE